I0122151

EVOLVING PASSERBY

LIVING IN ALIGNMENT

YAEL GOJMAN

EVOLVING PASSERBY
Living in Alignment

Edited by Hellen Soriano
Cover photo by Roberto Nickson from Pexels
Cover Design by Sandra Schwartzman
www.SSWDesign.com

CONTENTS

FOREWORD

I met Yael a few years ago when we were both living in Vietnam. She is a native Spanish speaker, and I will always have a bit of a fascination with the language, so we met weekly at a café to converse. It almost immediately became clear to me that Yael was a very special person.

This became apparent not only through our topics of conversation, but also through her entire demeanor. Above all, she is passionate, loving, and down-to-earth. I believe these qualities, combined with her personal history, give her a lot to share with the world at large.

Yael questions life while analyzing her own. Nobody knows the answers to life's bigger questions, but Yael has always taken it upon herself to attempt to work out how to live in alignment with her values, even if those values and beliefs are constantly evolving, which she gives them permission to do (a very important concept!). Through her story, she will inspire you to do the same.

Everyone has different experiences. Everyone's situation is different. However, I believe that we all experience the same basic feelings, whether they are fleeting or super intense. We also can all relate to each other in some ways. The stories Yael shares about her life are relevant to anyone and everyone because we all deal with some sort of hardships. This book will encourage you to question and analyze your past, present, and future. You will learn how to accept what has already happened, get comfortable with trying again, and always keep learning. You will see that sometimes we don't learn from our mistakes the first time around, and that's okay. Instead, we can continue to take risks and push ourselves to new levels.

The fullness of her life up to this point gives Yael all the creditability she needs. Summing up all that has happened to her and where she is now is incredible—she has experienced so much in a relatively short time, and what's more is that she takes the time to reflect and explore who she is in a way that is thought-provoking and immensely helpful to us as readers.

It is my sincere hope that you, like me, will have many takeaway points that will allow you to live a life full of love, learning, and faith in the journey.

Yvette Smith

INTRODUCTION

The journey of self-discovery is one of the most challenging and confronting, yet extraordinary, exciting, and rewarding ones we can ever take on. We think we know something about ourselves -about our traits, likes, priorities, preferences, etc. - and we may suddenly find ourselves in situations that come to challenge everything we ever thought we knew to be true. I imagine this to be the case for everyone, but not wanting to assume, I will speak only for myself.

This has undoubtedly been the case, particularly over the past seventeen years, ever since I graduated from high school. During my senior year, I had a mental image of what I thought my life would be like: I would take a leap year and go to Israel, then I would return to Mexico and start my graphic design studies. At some point, I would get married, have kids, and live happily ever after. Little did I realize at that time, that this 'life-plan' was not really my own; it was one that had been drilled into my brain by my family, my community, and by society in general, as the way life was *supposed* to be.

If I look further back into my teenage years, I can definitely point out multiple times during which I felt like I was different. I did not enjoy the same activities that most people my age enjoyed. I was never a big fan of drinking or going out to clubs. I did not enjoy the same types of conversations

1

either; I used to feel rather uncomfortable when my friends gossiped, yet it seemed to be a common pastime among people our age.

Perhaps to you, this does not seem to be a big deal. People are different and that is perfectly acceptable. To me, it was an ongoing source of struggle. I did not have the wisdom or confidence to define my preferences as valid as the other ones. Instead, and for the longest time, I used to believe that there was something wrong with me.

It has taken many years of very deep inner work, along with plenty of profound life experiences for me to start to *own* those differences, and to embrace them as beautiful and magical elements that make me a unique and extraordinary human being - just like everyone else is, in their own way.

Now, I would like to share what this journey has been like for me in many different areas of my life, along with the greatest lessons I have learned in the process. And I would like to empower you to pursue your own journey with confidence. I am extremely aware that there are elements that could hinder one's desire and willingness to follow this journey. I am also absolutely certain that there is nothing more valuable, life-altering, or fulfilling than ongoingly *discovering* Who You Really Are and daring to live your life *in complete alignment* with it.

There are aspects of Who I Am that I totally was not aware of, as you will find out. Those were indeed a discovery. However, there were a few others that I intuitively knew, but for the longest time did not have the courage to own and live by.

When I say 'Who You Really Are' I don't necessarily mean that we exist in a set way that we are out to uncover. What I mean is that in every moment we hold a vision of who we are -of what we are like, what we are capable of, what our purpose is, etc.- and this vision changes as our consciousness rises. Thus, everything we experience in life becomes a new opportunity for us to discover and experience ourselves as being closer to that vision.

While this journey has been going on for many years already, it only started coming to fruition in more meaningful ways the moment I became willing to pay the costs that would come with living in alignment with Who I Am. Even though I don't expect this book to magically implant that courage and disposition, I do intend that, by joining in my journey, you will develop a sense of safety and confidence to know that it is OKAY to explore and pursue your own.

FACING AND CHALLENGING SELF-LIMITING BELIEFS

"An unquestioned mind is the world of suffering"
- Byron Katie.

How we operate as human beings is pretty straight forward, in terms of mechanics. We have a thought or belief about something, we figure out a way to find evidence to support that this belief is true, and then we modify our behavior to make sure it is consistent with it. We don't always do this consciously; many of these thoughts or beliefs are actually blind spots for us, and we find our lives being driven by these, without even knowing they are there.

A large part of our suffering stems from us not identifying the existence of such beliefs, or even if we do, from not questioning or daring to challenge them. What I am going to share here are some of the self-limiting beliefs I used to hold growing up, many of which remained loud and present for way too many years. Each of these used to rob me of my power and kept me small in a different area of my life. It has only been through a thorough, persistent, and relentless commitment to putting in the work to become the best version of myself, that I have slowly been able to get to the source of -and transform- aspects of my being that were holding me back.

4

As I thought of writing this chapter, I was hoping that I would be able to talk about each and every one of these as absolute victories and disempowering thoughts that no longer showed up. And this was my hope mostly because I thought that I needed to portray "a perfect image" with "the perfect and proven recipe for success" in order for this book to be worth reading. It was after working through this self-limiting belief that I realized that the beauty of vulnerability lies not in showing that we have it all figured out, but in sharing our struggles and the effort we are putting in to get past them. If I appear as 'having it all together', my story may intimidate you more than inspire you. Yet, if I share myself openly, it may give you a greater sense of normalcy and the strength to keep working, knowing that, as Jim Kwik says:

"Practice makes Progress "

It's funny that I would quote him here because he is an expert in learning and memory - he works on transforming limiting beliefs as a *means* to unlock people's brainpower, not as an *end*. However, this specific statement has been extremely empowering for me because my whole life I had heard that *"Practice makes Perfect"* which used to set a seemingly unattainable standard. One that caused more frustration and disappointment than good.

My mom has repeatedly told me that there are three factors we can consider when determining whether there has been any progress in different areas of life, which can be utilized to assess the prevalence of self-limiting beliefs.

1) Do they show up with the same *frequency* as they used to? Are they things that are roaming in my mind

every day, multiple times a day? Or do they show up more seldomly?
2) Do they affect me with the same *intensity* when they show up? Do I get as worked up and as paralyzed by them as I did in the past?
3) When they do show up, and they affect me, does the effect have the same *duration* as it used to? Perhaps before it would paralyze me for weeks or months and now only for a few hours.

I invite you to keep these points in mind as you read through my beliefs, or if any of yours pop up as you read, to acknowledge the work and progress that you have achieved rather than putting yourself down for not having attained perfection.

Having said all of this, it is not particularly relevant to talk about where these beliefs stemmed from. Instead, I will share *how* these used to limit me and what allowed me to transform them to the extent that I have: how I have managed to make progress in the frequency, intensity, and duration with which they show up.

Remember! Challenging self-limiting beliefs, just like everything else in life, is a work in progress.

BELIEF I: I am incompetent. I can't think critically, solve problems or be resourceful

Growing up, I wouldn't readily take on any leadership roles. And if I did, I would doubt myself every single step of the way, discreetly passing on the power and responsibility to someone who I was supposed to be *sharing it* with whenever possible. This was the case, for example, when I became a leader in the Girl Scouts. Another girl and I were in charge of a group of teenagers for two years, and we needed to come up with weekly themes and activities that would transmit a valuable message that was aligned with the principles of being a Scout. Even today, I can vividly remember this belief running my actions and my conversations during that time, turning a period that could have been fun and enjoyable into a challenging and troublesome experience.

Fast forward some twelve years. I registered to take a two-year Team, Management, and Leadership program, in which we were trained to gain mastery in these three distinctions; the creation of teams and teamwork; what/how to manage them to produce results (managing promises versus people) and developing ourselves and supporting others to be effective and extraordinary leaders. The program was divided into quarters, and in each quarter, participants were encouraged to take on different accountabilities that would support the whole team in accomplishing the outcomes we sought.

The way in which I experienced the belief of being incompetent during this program was that during the first two

7

quarters I would either not take any accountabilities, or I would, but would have a terrible emotional breakdown halfway through that would result in someone else taking it over. Not knowing how to do it and not believing I was capable of figuring it out was mortifying to me. It was easier to break down into tears and manipulate everyone around me into believing I was unable to be responsible for this task when what I should have done is take it on properly and learn to work through it. I had forgotten that the program was a training ground for me to be able to try, make mistakes, and try again, in a safe, loving, and supportive environment.

This belief started to transform when I went into the third quarter and took on the accountability of Logistics, which was the one responsible for making sure that every single one of the team members had a plane ticket and a hotel room booked, and all the meals ordered for the following course weekend we would have at the end of the quarter. It seemed intimidating initially, but somehow this time I managed to stick through it and not want to quit halfway through. I was very impressed with myself with how much and how well I was able to get it done. I think that was the first time that I began to realize that I won't ever know what I am capable of doing until I give it a proper try, and, that once I commit to giving it a try, I will be surprised with my own abilities and also by the extraordinary people I will find that will support me to make it happen.

From then on, I have taken on many other projects and responsibilities that the old me would have never accepted, such as seriously exploring the possibility of becoming an inventor, presenting new ideas and programs at my job, or even writing this book. It has been a gradual process, and I admit that the belief may still show up sometimes. However, the difference now is that it no longer stops me from taking action.

Something that inspired me to dare to start taking on greater responsibilities than those I thought I was capable of was this phrase I was told over and over again during my participation in that and many other programs:

"Step into the listening of others"

We all have a little voice in our heads that is constantly judging and assessing everything we do and everything that is going on within or around us. Often, what it says is not necessarily flattering or empowering, and its opinion of who we are or what we are capable of accomplishing tends to be quite critical and limiting. In contrast, and because other people's perception of us has not been tainted by our own self-judgment and skewed interpretation of events, they tend to have a much greater "listening" of us, of who we are and of what we can achieve. Thus, during that period of my life, it was extremely helpful for me to be surrounded by people who had a more generous and objective listening of me than the one I had of myself.

However, as time has gone by and my level of self-awareness has continued to rise, I have become more capable -funny that I would use this word- to *see* and *own* these abilities and resourcefulness. I may still be initially intimidated by a new, unfamiliar task or challenge at hand. Yet, I have now experienced over and over again that all it takes is for me to:

a) Be committed to making something happen

9

b) *Know* that the way and timing in which it happens will always be perfect
c) *Know* that I will always have what I need and I am always taken care of (by G-d, the universe or a Greater Power, however I understand it)

With these three elements present, the *How* will unravel itself. Perhaps the end result won't even look the way I initially imagined it, but boy! will the journey to making it happen be an extraordinary, fulfilling, and growth-promoting one.

BELIEF II: I am not capable of accomplishing anything big. I can only make a difference in the lives of a few people; I do not have what it takes to do it on a grand scale

This is an interesting one because what led to a shift in this belief was not necessarily a dramatic change in the physical reality but rather a new realization at a metaphysical level. Let me explain. Before 2011, which is when I started to get involved in personal growth and development programs, I did not think of myself as someone who had anything to contribute to anyone, period. Since I started on this path, however, each program I took created a new opening in my perspective of what was possible for me both on an individual and on a community or global level.

At the end of that year, I took a Self-Expression and Leadership Program during which I needed to create and take actions towards making a project that would positively impact one of my circles of influence, it could be related to my family, friends, work, fitness, etc. The idea was for me to get it started and then give it away so that it would take a life of its own and have a much greater reach which would not depend on me to exist.

The community I chose to work with was parents of children with special needs, which was the population I was professionally working with at the time. I named the project "Because You Matter". The idea was to acknowledge the parents of these kids for the magnificent effort, patience, and dedication they pour into their kids on a daily basis and let them know that what they do does not go unnoticed nor is taken for granted. My team and I successfully created three community events that turned out to be moving and empowering for these parents and the community attended. Afterward, I wanted to turn "Because You Matter" into something greater that could help them -and thousands of other parents- get access to equipment or services that could improve both the quality of their kids' lives and their own even further. Sadly, this did not turn out as expected.

Sometime after "Because You Matter" had died off in that form, I came up with a new idea for it to exist that was related to health and wellbeing, and having accountability partners for whatever each participant stated to be important to them. My vision was to partner up with a certain number of people, let's say three, each of which would take two or three more people on, and so forth, and it could have a huge ripple effect. The idea sounded great, but in execution, it wasn't very successful. I ended up becoming the single accountability partner for a little over one hundred people at some point, and this was not sustainable for me nor was it multiplying the way I had intended. So, despite my greatest reach having been little over a hundred, nowadays there are only four of us playing.

Just as with these examples, I had a few different initiatives, and while I know each of those made a difference in at least one person's life, the idea of me being someone who touches the lives of thousands or millions of people continued to seem unattainable.

For a long time, my problem was that I was comparing myself to others, and to other global and famous projects that had been launched from the same programs I had participated in. This had created an expectation of what 'making a difference' needed to look like, and because it wasn't showing up the exact way I intended it to, I was convinced it was not happening at all.

This was the case until I started opening up to the world of metaphysics and formulated my own understanding of what making a difference in someone's life needed -or did not need- to look like. I used to think that it had to be either direct interaction with or direct participation in any of the projects I was coming up with, in the sense that failure to do either one meant no impact at all. However, I came to realize that by the mere fact of having an interaction with someone, no matter how small it is, we could make a positive difference in that person's life. Even if it is just offering a heartwarming smile that comes during a difficult time, or saying hi and acknowledging their presence in a moment when they happen to be feeling lonely, those little things do have a positive effect on others.

By touching one person's life, even in the smallest way, we may cause a shift in the way they behave and interact with other people in their lives, which is indirectly impacting the other people's lives also, and that continues to be paid forward. It can definitely be noticed more when it is done in an intentional, measurable way, for example by participating in programs or charities that have a specific social impact. But that does not mean that it does not occur otherwise. If we think about it from this perspective, we will never really know the number of lives that we have touched, nor is it really important for us to know.

Keeping this perspective in mind, and making it a point to make sure every single interaction I have with other human beings is a loving, generous, kind, compassionate and respectful one, I can simply stand in *knowing* that the impact is way greater than I will ever know. In addition, for as long as I am alive, I have the opportunity to continue coming up with -and launching- ideas that may increase the number of lives I empower. And this book is yet another one of those.

What I want to leave you with, in terms of this belief, is that there is no 'set' or 'unique' way in which things can exist or be accomplished.

BELIEF III: I cannot read books and will never be a reader

This is one of my favorite ones! When I was a student in elementary, middle, and high school, I did not enjoy reading at all. It was a struggle every time I was assigned to read a book because it would take so much for me to be able to concentrate! I would read one line and my mind would have drifted already, so I had to go back and read it over and over again. Or I would start reading, and about fifteen minutes into it my eyes would start feeling very heavy and I would pass out. It was annoying, frustrating, and an ongoing reminder of how much I sucked at it.

There were a few books that I managed to read, and that I actually enjoyed, such as Memoirs of a Geisha by Arthur Golden, or To Kill a Mockingbird by Harper Lee, but it took me forever to finish them. Around the time that Harry Potter came out and everyone was obsessed with it, my best friend kept encouraging me to read it, but it became a joke for us because, for the life of me, I couldn't get past the first couple of chapters. I was absolutely certain that being someone who could read constantly, who would finish books [relatively] quickly and who would look forward to grabbing the next one was never going to be my case. However, it was a dream I always had. I always wanted to be someone who would devour books and information, and who couldn't get enough of it because of the expanded world perspectives it afforded.

Because reading was something I so badly wanted to be able to do, I explored different factors that could be limiting my ability to do it, such as my eye health, my ability to process visual information, etc. I will first share my experience in relationships with these two, and then reveal what ended up making the biggest difference.

My vision was always perfectly clear, so I never thought of getting my eyes checked until I was in my mid-twenties. I went to see an optometrist, who prescribed some vision therapy to strengthen my eyes because he said that my ability to converge was weak. I did that for a couple of months. He also prescribed some reading glasses, and I was able to read for a little longer, but the change was not significant.

I used those same glasses for about six or seven years until I started to experience significant eye strain, so I thought I needed to update my prescription. To make a long story short, I visited four or five different specialists between Vietnam and Mexico, each of which told me a different story (you need a little more prescription, you need a *lot* more, you need *no* prescription, etc.) which drove me crazy. I ended up seeing an ophthalmologist who, by the way, is my brother's friend, and he told me; "no matter what anyone else has told you before, you have perfect vision, you *do not need* to wear glasses, what you are dealing with are some allergies, so let's attend to that". It has been nine months since I stopped wearing glasses altogether and I have been able to read with no problem.

If my problem was not stemming from eye-related issues, what was causing it? Here are a few possible answers:

a) I was forcing myself to read certain types of books or topics that I was not particularly interested in.
b) I was always exposed -or had access- to endless other things that could occupy my time, so I had never made reading a priority.

15

c) I had strongly ingrained limiting beliefs about my ability to read that had not been questioned.
d) I was never really properly trained on *how* to read.

In September of 2018, I went to India and participated in a ten-day Introduction to Buddhism silent retreat. Those ten days were the most significant in transforming my relationship with reading for two main reasons: The first one is that I was truly fascinated with the topics I was learning about, and I wanted to understand more, which took care of the first answer above. This means that the moment I found something I was interested in, there was nothing that could stop me from digging deeper into it.

The second one was that, because it was a mostly silent retreat (except for our ability to ask questions during the lectures or have an hour-long discussion with a group per day) I had *a lot* of time on my hands. Thus, I would carry my books with me and read in between meditation and lecture sessions, during meals, or basically any time I was free. Since we were not allowed to have our phones or computers with us, books became my main source of entertainment and allowed me to enjoyably pass the time.

By the end of the ten days, I had discovered I was someone who was deeply interested in Buddhist philosophy and psychology, and who deeply enjoyed spending time in silence, in nature, and reading. I feel like this was one of those instances in life in which it may not necessarily be that I did not enjoy reading before, but I simply did not *know* that I enjoyed it because I had never given myself the opportunity to do it without having my mind rushing into the next activity. This time to myself was one of the most beautiful gifts I could have gotten because it unintentionally also came to challenge and "prove wrong" my former disempowering belief, all of which I am forever grateful for.

After the retreat, I started reading much more, but still not with the consistency or at the level I would have wanted to. Almost a year later, however, I bumped into a course online called "Super Reading" by Jim Kwik that seemed to be exactly what I needed. Without hesitation, I signed up for it. One of the most fundamental shifts that this course provided stemmed from the following quote:

"There is no such thing as a Good or Bad [memory], there is only a Trained or Untrained one" (You can substitute the word 'memory' with the word 'reader', 'student', 'professional, etc.)

Understanding that it was not so much a matter of being gifted -or not- with certain skills, but rather a matter of how properly trained I had been on them, took a huge weight off my shoulders and opened up a clear new course of action. The question was no longer whether I could ever be good at something, but rather what I needed to be properly trained on, and practice consistently, to be able to perform at the level I would like to.

Thanks to Jim Kwik's teachings, not only did I become a lot more comfortable with reading, but I also began to unlock my brain's potential and found myself capable of reading and learning much more than I ever believed possible. Within the seven months following those training programs, I read about thirteen books, something completely unprecedented based on my reading history. As you can imagine, I was completely over the moon!

A few years ago, I learned to ask this question when positive things happen in my life:

"How does it get any better than this/that?"

I believe it invites even better things to happen. I would be lying if I told you that I clearly understand the reasoning behind asking this question because I am not very familiar with Access Consciousness, which is where it comes from. However, it feels good to use it, so I have made it a part of my life, and I have noticed that better and better things have continued to happen.

Why am I telling you this now? Because I was extremely happy with the results from those reading programs and wondered how it could get even better. This is what happened afterward: when the Pandemic of the Coronavirus hit Southeast Asia, I was living in Vietnam and chose to take advantage of the time I wasn't allowed to work to travel to Mexico and visit my family. I was staying at my mom's place and walked to visit the rest of my family regularly. During my walks, I would notice a sign above a storefront that read "Are you tired of not having anyone to discuss what you read with?". It caught my attention, so I walked in to see what it was about. It turned out to be a center that trains people on how to read and learn optimally, more effectively, and more efficiently.

How was this one better than the one I had already taken? The one I had taken had been fully online, following daily videos for twenty-one days, so I could gauge my progress but there was no one really monitoring it. In

18

contrast, in this new program, I have daily practices at home and weekly meetings with a facilitator who assesses my progress and determines if I can move onto the next level. Their promise and guarantee are that by the end of the four-to-eight month course (depending on the speed at which I advance through the modules) I will be reading ten times faster and will have one hundred percent comprehension. I cannot yet imagine what that would be like, but I can't wait to find out. In the meantime, I have managed to progressively challenge and transform the limiting belief I had around the topic.

BELIEF IV: I have a learning disability that I am really good at compensating for, and that's why nobody has noticed

I was a pretty decent student my whole life, but I always attributed that to the fact that the academic demands that were placed on me were not too high. I managed to get through my whole schooling experience waking up at four in the morning on the day of the test, cramming all the information in, doing well on it, and then forgetting everything I had studied. Books we needed to read or papers we needed to write were assigned with plenty of time, and I would often leave everything for the last minute but still somehow manage to have something acceptable to hand in. I always felt that the way I operated was off but, because my grades were good, nobody really paid much attention to it.

When I was in Israel and I tried to keep up with more advanced notetaking and recalling of information, it felt even more evident to me that there was something wrong with my ability to learn or perform academically. This situation was partially what led to my first depressive episode that resulted in me going back to Mexico. When I started receiving psychological and psychiatric treatment for depression, I was also prescribed something to support me with my attention and concentration deficits. I can't recall how long I took that medication, but it seemed to help me get through my associate's and bachelor's degrees, both of which demanded yet a greater level of performance.

I was able to successfully complete both of these degrees without a depressive relapse. However, I found myself feeling close to having one many times because, even if I did not leave the assignments until the last minute, it did take me hours and hours to get them done. It did not feel normal that it would take so long, or that I needed to read everything so many times. It felt like my processing speed was significantly slower than other people's. At some point, I got a professional evaluation done and it showed that, while my intellectual quotient was great, it indeed took me three times as long and I needed to apply twice as much effort as other people to get certain things done.

The cognitive and emotional effort I needed to do the assignments was high. What I was not able - or willing- to see was that the time invested was directly proportional to the quality of the work I delivered. I was forging the ground towards becoming a comfortable, clear, and effective writer. Perhaps my writing is no longer based on papers I write or books I read. However, I do believe that my ability to integrate information and ideas and compile them in a way that makes sense and can be easily understood has significantly improved as a result of the amount of time I dedicated to studying and writing back in the day.

Basically, it was a matter of reframing the situation. The facts were the same: I was devoting the same large amounts of time to learning. However, the interpretation shifted: it went from it being "because I am too slow" to "I am building and practicing a skill I did not have before, that's allowing me to become a much more effective learner". For example, it was not until I started school in Florida that I discovered flow charts as an extraordinary tool to visualize and understand the connection between the elements being studied. It was then then that I learned that, based on how I learn best, I *need* to see where each element fits in the larger picture in order to make sense of it. It is a simple detail, right? But I believe that having known this when I was in middle school or high school could have made it easier for me to grasp and retain information and made studying more enjoyable.

Going back to what I mentioned before about there not being good or bad learners but rather trained or untrained ones, I realize that I was never properly taught *HOW* to study; I was basically given the material and told "okay, you have to learn this for the test" and I was left to figure it out on my own. Interestingly enough, this was not just the case at the school that I went to; I think it is quite a common problem that people face all over the world. I have personally witnessed that in Vietnam, where I have been teaching for a few years now, it is very evident that students struggle with the same obstacle.

In short, I was able to gradually transform my belief regarding my learning abilities through diligent work and the exploration of methodologies that suit my needs better. I firmly believe that a lot of the frustration and desperation I experienced on this topic could have been avoided had various approaches to learning been introduced to me and actively put into practice over the years. That way, I could have built my toolbox with a lot of methods to use and made my learning experience easier and more enjoyable.

I strongly encourage you or anyone you know who has or works with children, to make it a priority to invest time and resources into teaching them *how to learn* early on, so that they have a solid and positive experience with learning going forward. After all, defining ourselves as capable/smart and properly equipped does not only affect our academic performance, but also our self-image and how we interact with the world.

BELIEF V: I will never be good at playing the piano

When I was in elementary school, I used to take organ lessons at home. I was fairly good at playing by ear but had a really hard time reading the notes. The teacher would get upset at me almost every week because I wouldn't do my homework. After a few years of this dynamic, I stopped the lessons and forgot about the idea of playing an instrument for a really long time.

Fast forward, in 2013 I met a couple with whom I eventually became pretty close. The guy is an extraordinary dueling pianist and is one of the most talented musicians I have ever met. I was fascinated by his abilities, and spending time with him and seeing how much he enjoyed playing made me realize that it was something I was also very passionate about and really wanted to be able to do, but did not think I was capable of.

About two years after I met him, we started having conversations about him teaching me how to play the electric keyboard. In the beginning, he used to come to my house and teach me in person, but sometime later we switched to phone lessons, and according to him, I was making very impressive progress. It turned out, once again, that *how* something is taught can make all the difference between getting it or not getting it. His teaching method and the books he used seemed to work for me. I was very pleased.

I was already on a roll with my progress, when suddenly everything changed -I separated from my second husband and started traveling the world-, and for the next six or seven months did not play again. Once I settled in Vietnam, I searched for an electric keyboard, which was quite an adventure due to the language barrier, and took on the challenge of continuing to learn on my own.

I started practicing with a software that gave me instant feedback on the notes I was playing -whether they were correct or not- which turned out to be pretty effective, and I made nice progress with it. However, I mistakenly relied on this feedback too much and wasn't making the conscious effort to practice actually reading the notes.

Nevertheless, I was able to play songs that I never thought I would.

Once again, my progress got interrupted by my six-month trip in 2018. I was a bit frustrated about my circumstantial lack of continuity, because, as much as I could practice whenever I found a piano somewhere, it was nothing like practicing every day at home the way I had been doing for quite some time. By the time my trip ended, in February 2019, I was certain I had forgotten almost everything I had learned. To my surprise, that was not the case. I was able to pick it back up, this time without the need for the software, and continued to make very decent progress.

While I find my progress interrupted again now, because I have been out of Vietnam for a few months due to the Coronavirus and I do not currently have access to a keyboard, there are a few different lessons that I have learned from this journey.

1) Consistency is THE key, to learning an instrument -or anything else, for that matter. There is *no* way for us to do something consistently and not make progress. Perhaps the progress won't be at the pace we would like, but we will always be moving forward.
2) Being generous with ourselves is important. I kept comparing myself to the level of skill my friend has, and making myself worry for being nowhere near. What I failed to take into account is that he has had forty-plus more years of practice and experience than I do. When we are learning something new, we

should not compare ourselves to anyone else's performance but rather to how we were doing when we first started, and give ourselves credit for it.

3) Sometimes, when I feel like I am hitting a wall, rather than keep trying and getting frustrated, it is better to step away and take a break for a few hours or even a day. It happened to me many times that I was practicing something over and over again and feeling like "I wasn't getting it", and then I would step away for a day or so and get back to it, only to realize that the time had served my brain to "assimilate" the skill.

I do not know if I will ever be as good of a pianist as some of the musicians I admire, especially because I don't dedicate that much of my time to it, and those levels of performance require hours and hours of practice. However, I do know I can certainly continue to improve. And that the same principle applies to anything else I may want to learn in my life.

In addition, there is a quote by Ralph Waldo Emerson that I really appreciate:

"It's not the destination; it is the journey"

What's most important and relevant for me is not whether or not I have become a professional piano player, but rather everything I have done, grown, and learned about myself in the process of becoming a better one... And it has been an extraordinary adventure.

BELIEF VI: I don't have what it takes to be financially independent and/or successful

This belief is one that resulted in me making a few life decisions that did not turn out to be the smartest ones: I started college in Israel rather than travel the world -which is what I really wanted to do- because I did not think I would be able to sustain myself if I lost my parents' and the government's financial support. Then I rushed into having the one who became my second husband move in with me because I did not think I would be able to manage my expenses otherwise. While many -actually most- people my age at the time in Israel or in the States held jobs to complement their expenses, the mere thought of me having to recall an order and bring out a tray with food or drinks seemed like an unattainable task. It sounds ridiculous, and yet it was so real and intimidating to me! I was certain that I would not be able to learn even the most basic skills to perform the simplest job.

Once I started working, as an English teacher in Mexico or an Occupational Therapy Assistant in Florida, I was making money but always feeling like I had no negotiating skills and was simply 'taking what I was being offered', when I could have potentially asked for more. For the longest time, I was certain that the only way I could ever earn some income -or consider having financial abundance or success- depended on the amount of money I could make per hour, and the number of hours I could work per week. And since those two were limited by my professional skill-level and the number of hours I was willing to work every week, then I was never going to be someone who had an abundance of money.

For some reason, I was never willing to have a second job and work more than 40 hours, even if that meant me having to limit myself more with my expenses. In my mind, I was bound to always worry about money and always depend on someone else to support me financially.

Things began to shift when I went on my trip to Southeast Asia and started considering the possibility of staying there long-term. I had a mortgage to pay every month, a car lease, some credit card debt, student and personal loans...How was I going to manage it all?

This is one of those circumstances where the famous quote *"where there is a will, there is a way"* comes in handy. I was so committed to continuing living my dream now that I had finally started living it, that I was going to do whatever it took to make it happen. Two of my bedrooms in Florida were already being rented, and I managed to get the third one rented out as well. I got my car lease partially taken over, and simultaneously I managed to find a way to live in Vietnam for six weeks while I prepared to get the TESOL (Teaching English to Speakers of Other Languages) certification to be able to start properly teaching, without paying for accommodation by volunteering in an English center. I arranged to receive financial support to get a laptop to complete the certification, and two months later I was able to start working.

All of the above were sources of abundance - whether it was from the money I was getting or the money I was not having to spend- that absolutely did not depend on however much I could make per hour or however many hours I was willing to work. I found that astounding! And so it was that my experience and understanding of wealth creation and abundance in life began to shift.

Once I settled in Vietnam and started working, I realized that abundance did not depend on making much more money either. My monthly income had been reduced to half of what it used to be, perhaps, and yet, by the end of 2017 I had already paid off a large part of my personal loans and all of my credit card debt. How could that happen with such a noticeable reduction in income? Well, the cost of living is significantly lower in Vietnam than anywhere else I had ever lived in, so the money went much further.

Most recently, I completed an extraordinary program called Lifebook, through which I got clarity on what my beliefs, vision, purpose, and strategies are in each one of twelve different categories, to live the life of my dreams. Particularly in the Finances category, I experienced a radical shift because I discovered a new and empowering belief to substitute the one about my wealth being dependent on the number of hours I put in:

*"Wealth is an Effect, the Cause is value creation;
the more I increase the value I bring and the contribution I
make, inevitably the greater my wealth will be as well"*

I may not be the most financially savvy person out there, but I certainly have a lot to contribute and I also have an ongoing commitment to becoming a better version of myself, which inevitably increases my value. Thus, despite facing small drawbacks in the process to grow my finances -such as being out of work for a few months due to the

Coronavirus- I now *know* that a wealthier and even more abundant future awaits.

BELIEF VII: I can't push myself physically (can't run, lift, climb, or dance)

My whole life, up until maybe two years ago, I was seemingly physically active, but not really. Let me explain what I mean. Ever since I can remember, I used to participate in sports classes. The very first one, at the age of three, was swimming lessons. Then, I joined gymnastics, track and field, aerobics, tennis, volleyball, soccer, traditional Jewish dances, etc. I always showed up for my classes, but I also always managed to get distracted with friends and socialize, or "had to go get some water" or "had something important to take care of" the moment my heart rate started rising.

I hated the feeling of my body warming up inside, so I used to come up with great excuses and/or use my charming personality to get out of having to push myself. This worked for me because I did not have to push myself too much, but it did not work for me because the disempowering feeling I experienced towards those unpleasant sensations stayed with me through the years and made me really anxious at the mere thought of exerting my body a little more than I thought I could handle.

When I graduated high school and went to Israel, traditionally many of my friends joined a two-month program called Marva, which is a little taste of what being in the Israeli

Defense Forces is like. It was also a great opportunity to challenge yourself and push your limits physically and maybe emotionally as well. While those who took part in it loved the experience, the mere thought of the conditions and physical demands that would be placed on me terrified me enough that I chose not to do that program, and to do a volunteering one instead, in which my job was cleaning certain areas or serving food.

In the following years, I was still somewhat active, but without pushing myself too much. I got into yoga and started learning how to dance salsa, but neither activity was too demanding. Then, in 2014 my second husband and I got into a phase of wanting to be as healthy as possible, and so he bartered services with a personal trainer who started coming to the house. He was amazing, and tremendously patient with me. He knew that my anxiety would come up if he pushed me too much and was okay with dealing with some tears and supporting me during the training. I can't remember why we only trained with him for some months, but when we stopped, my old self-limiting beliefs around exercise reared back up.

My greatest accomplishment after that period was to run and finish a 5k. This was totally unprecedented, and I couldn't figure out how, mentally speaking, I managed to do it, since I know my greatest barrier was always in my mind. But I did.

Fast forward to 2017. When I moved to Vietnam, I had a lot of time in my hands every day. I only worked about twenty hours per week, so I decided to use part of that spare time to work on my health and fitness. I alternated between swimming -which was lots of fun and I pushed myself to swim distances I never thought possible for me- and going to the gym and trying to figure out what to do there because I had no experience or knowledge on the topic. I met a guy who happened to be a trainer, and who said he would be opening his own gym in the near future. A few months later, after realizing that I could only advance and push myself so far on my own, I reached out to him and started training with him three or four times a week. He was absolutely extraordinary! He never bought into my smallness. I would always say "you're crazy if you think I can lift that, or if you think I can do it so many times" and he would say to me "you're much stronger than you think you are, believe me, I know what I am doing". He was right every single time.

One of the things that he used to do that motivated me to push myself, even more, was the fact that he knew that I loved piano music. Thus, when we were in the middle of a training session and he saw that I was starting to struggle emotionally -because the anxiety and fear of not being able continued to show up for a while- he would turn some piano music on. It was an unspoken way of encouraging me that moved me and made me want to try harder.

He got me to lift amounts of weight and perform exercises that seemed impossible to me; he supported me in creating the discipline and a way to thoroughly enjoy working out so that doing so was no longer something I "needed" to do, but something I was looking forward to doing. In the beginning, I would only show up at the gym because I knew he was waiting for me. Nowadays, I do so because I know that my body feels so much better when I do. Potentially I would push myself even more if I continued to work with him as often as I used to, but I nevertheless do so much more on my own now than I ever thought I would.

The thought of marathons or triathlons or more demanding sports still seems intimidating. I admire those who effortlessly participate in them. However, and unlike many years ago, now I also know that, if participating in any of those events was something that suddenly became a priority for me, I would be able to do it.

It has taken a lot of perseverance and resilience to keep trying. I feel like I have been blessed to find someone who knows *how* to support me to work through it while being committed to living a healthy life. As you can probably tell, I am still not in a place of one-hundred-percent confidence, and telling you otherwise would come from wanting to look good in front of you, wanting to seem as if though "I've fully overcome this belief" which is not quite the case yet. However, I accept this as part of my life process and acknowledge the efforts and the progress I have accomplished so far.

Where can you do the same thing? Is there something you do with more -or less- frequency, intensity, or duration than before? I invite you to acknowledge every step forward you've taken, no matter how small, and remind yourself that as easy as it is to compare ourselves to others, the greatest and most empowering assessment we can make is about whether we have made progress *from where we used to be.*

BELIEF VIII: I am 100% responsible for anything that happens -or does not happen- in my life

Up until the time when I was twenty-six years old, I never really thought much about responsibility for anything. If I had to guess, I would say that I used to unconsciously place all the responsibility for everything that happened or did not happen in my life out there. Almost as if I was the victim of circumstances, of people, and of the world. It did not serve me very well to live that way, but I did not know any better.

It was at that point when I started to get involved in personal growth and development and started to be able to see "blind spots" of certain beliefs, attitudes, and behaviors I had that were driving my life and taking all my power away. My most prominent behavior was that of always asking everyone for their opinion or advice on personal matters, naively believing that if I followed what they suggested, the responsibility of the consequences would fall on them, not on me. I was able to distinguish this tendency and started to turn it around, coming from the perspective that: "If I take full responsibility for the decisions I make and for my relationships and everything in my life, it puts me in a position where I can do something about it. If I put the responsibility out there, I am merely at the mercy of others or of whatever happens".

I adopted this new place to stand, but I took it literally, to the extent of being extremely hard on myself when things didn't turn out as intended. I soon forgot it was just a place to stand and not an absolute truth. I had also missed the fact that being responsible does not mean that it completely depends on me whether something actually happens or it does not, but rather that I do have a say on how I relate and respond to it. In an effort to live more empowered, I started applying my now-I-know skewed understanding of responsibility as much as possible in every area of my life. In many areas, it gave me a lot of power, but in many others, it actually took it away.

By this point, I was far from being spiritual. In fact, the mere thought of spirituality was overwhelming to me because of how abstract it is, so I did not even want to bother exploring or learning about it. Instead, I saw this cognitive approach (of taking one hundred percent responsibility) as a feasible alternative to living a more powerful life.

With time, I discovered that this was not fully doing it for me. Believing in 100% responsibility was causing a lot of stress and anxiety and was often leading to repeated feelings of failure and incompetence over circumstances that I didn't really have control over. Gradually, I began to open up to the possibility that there is a Greater Power - however I understand it- that also plays a role in how my life unfolds and in whether all the things I intend to do come to fruition or not. Progressively, my everyday life became a lot more peaceful and a new sense of trust in life developed.

I got, as a truth that works for *me*, that I can take all the actions and create all the ways of being I know, and even then, things will not always turn out the way I intended. And also, that there is a lot more power in being willing to *flow* and accept those 'detours' as perfect and part of a greater plan than there is in dueling on something and continuing to force things to happen.

From here on, when you see the word "action" I am referring to all three kinds: actions of the mind, body, and speech; what we think, do, and say respectively. I am fully responsible for taking all the actions I know to take. I am also totally responsible for *how* I respond to or deal with whatever happens or does not happen in my life. However, I am *not* responsible for how someone else perceives or deals with whatever actions I took or did not take, nor am I responsible for actions that other people choose to take or not to take. I can offer or put something in that I see missing if I believe it could make a difference in a given situation, or for a specific person. But ultimately, we are each in our individual journey, and respecting each other's timing and pace allows for a much greater, healthier, and empowering existence for all.

What I want to leave you with here is that it is valuable for us to be open to trying different beliefs or approaches to topics, but it is more so for us to trust our own judgment and ability to discern between beliefs that are empowering, those that are not, or those that *are* but not as an absolute. It has taken something from me to acknowledge that, while a given place to stand seems to have been extraordinarily effective for thousands of people -and even for me in certain situations-, it may not necessarily be the most effective or empowering one as "the truth" for my life.

It's okay to question, and it's okay to disagree. At the end of the day, there is no one-size-fits-all perspective, and as long as we are empowered and excited with the one we have taken on, and as long as we respect the other person's and we don't try to impose ours upon them, it does not really matter whether our perspective differs from those which the rest of the world holds.

BELIEF IX: I don't have any skills I am truly good at, the options of what I can do for a living are extremely limited

Boy! Has this one been a prevalent one! Having the tendency to compare myself to others, for years and years I managed to always be on the losing end of that comparison. *Everybody* was smarter, more creative, more talented, handier, more capable, more skilled, more resourceful, and more confident than me. There were a lot of things I was interested in, many of which I could do half-way but none that I was particularly good at to an extent that I could stand out or consider it an added asset to my personal toolbox.

I enjoy the arts -drawing, painting, or anything handmade- and I am pretty good at it when I am told what to do or how to do it, but if I need to come up with ideas on my own, my absurd need for perfection kicks in and blocks my creativity.

I am flexible and good at yoga, but not focused enough to recall sequences or be able to describe what each part of my body is doing in every pose. I simply do it but can't describe it. The same goes for weightlifting. I am pretty good at following directions and developing proper form but it's challenging for me to figure out routines or even correct my or someone else's posture during practice.

As I shared already, I was not a reader, so my general knowledge was on the weaker side, and slightly more complex topics -such as history, or spirituality- were too intimidating and I would avoid engaging or learning about them at all costs. I could hardly recall any facts about anything, names of songs or movies, lyrics... Math and Physics were too abstract and complex for me, the same goes for business and economy-related topics, and the list of perceived weaknesses could go on and on.

I was not fully aware of how many of those things I was so intimidated by could be developed and improved upon with intention, proper training, and consistency, but that is beyond the point. In my perspective, there was nothing that I was particularly good at, and when I had a conversation about that with my loved ones, I was always disappointed by their answers and I would end up feeling just as small.

They would say: "You are wonderful with people, you have an ability to connect and make people feel comfortable and loved, that is very unique". And I wanted to answer: "a) I don't know what about the way I relate to people is so special and b) that sounds like a nice thing you can say to try to make me feel better because, indeed, there's nothing else". They would also point languages as a strength, but I would find a way to play that down as well.

Somehow, I don't really know how, as the years have gone by, I have managed to start realizing that those two elements -the ability to connect with people and the skill for languages- along with the fact that I am so inquisitive, curious, open-minded, passionate, creative and eager to grow and be better, do make for a strong foundation that can open up a lot of opportunities for me.

I am still not sure I can point out the extent or the way in which these are important skills. In fact, the process of writing this part of the book has been a bit confronting because I notice that I am still not fully confident or capable of owning what my strengths are in the skill arena. However, if I consider the *frequency with which* this particular belief shows up, the *intensity* with which it affects me or limits me when it does, and the *duration* of its effects, I realize they have significantly decreased over time.

I will attribute this progress partially to all the inner work I continuously put into becoming a better version of myself, but also to my increased awareness and *knowing* that the universe is kind and that I am always taken care of. It does not matter so much whether I can name a long list of skills, as long as I pour my heart into anything I do -which I do- I will always find a way to make life work.

BELIEF X: I am worthless. I have to put up with less than I want. I should be grateful that someone wants to be with me (otherwise, I will most likely never find anyone to be with)

This belief is intense. Imagine how poorly I must have thought of myself, and how shocking it was for me to realize that this was a thought/belief that had been running my life! I am not sure when it started, but the earliest memory I have is from when I was in the seventh grade. There was a girl that I used to call my best friend, who said or did things that had me crying every-single-day. There are two particular instances that I look back on and ask myself "why the hell would I (or anyone) put up with something like that?" But then I understood that I did not think I deserved any better. I thought that at least I had someone I could call a friend after my former best friend had told me she did not want to be friends with me anymore, so it was better than nothing. It's not worth going into details, but I'm convinced it was a verbally and emotionally abusive friendship.

Four years later I started dating my first "serious" boyfriend, and how we got together had to do with the same sense of worthlessness. He had just come out of a relationship with a girl that he was head-over-heels in love with, and I happened to be "the next best thing" since she no longer wanted to be with him. But hey! Better to have a boyfriend that has someone else in his mind and heart, than to have no boyfriend at all! And I used to think that If I did not accept that relationship -or did not stay, despite all our differences- I wasn't going to find anyone else.

I graduated from high school, we broke up, and I left to go to Israel, where I met my first husband. The love and connection with him were profound from the very beginning, in actions, and in feelings, but not in words. For the longest time, he used to tell me "I do mean when I say I love you, but not in the way you are taking it". This element can not be strongly condemned because we did live in two different countries, and the fear and uncertainty of how we could ever manage to be together might have been what drove his words.

We made it happen; after three years of being long-distance, we found a way to be in the same place. In the following years, the relationship was quite peaceful and respectful. He appreciated me and made me feel deeply loved. However, a few years down the road, I started getting involved in personal growth. I changed, and our dynamics were no longer that great. We had strong differences of opinions. Part of this was caused by my belief that "the way I had discovered to go about life was the best and only way", but it resulted in some verbal abuse from his part as well. I remember instances when he said something to me that was disrespectful and got me very upset, and then he would follow up by asking if he could hug me and I would say yes.

Why would I say yes? Because I was still coming from that same belief. By that time, he was no longer treating me as well as I now know I deserve to be treated, nor was he accepting or supporting the fact that I was starting to find my own inner strength. However, he had already been putting up with a lot of my personal insecurities and emotional issues for years, and he still wanted to be with me, so I thought that if I did not take advantage of that, who knew if I could ever find anyone else that would be willing to put up with me all.

We ended up getting divorced. I entered the next relationship -which resulted in my second marriage- and it was pretty good overall, except that I rarely ever felt desired by him. The same thinking process showed up: we are great together, our communication is amazing, he knows how to support me with my insecurities and emotional breakdowns, he takes good care of me, I might as well take it -even though my sexual self-image is not being nurtured or satisfied- because I may otherwise never find anyone that's willing to be with me and put up with my flaws.

You probably get the point now of how I used to believe that they were almost doing me a favor by being with me, because of how difficult I was to be with and to love. There was also a recurring thought of "they give me so much and I bring so little to the relationship that I am lucky that despite it they want to stick around".

The problem with this last thought stemmed from the fact that I believed that giving love, affection, support, a safe space to grow, encouragement, a generous listening, family inclusion, attentiveness, and acknowledgment, was not as significant, let's say, as paying the bills, taking care of things around the house, helping solve problems or managing issues related to school, banks, insurances, and so forth. Those acts could be easily pointed out, whether mine were more abstract and could easily be overlooked, go unnoticed, or underacknowledged.

It took a few relationships and thirty-four years for me to start seeing and acknowledging what I bring to the table. Just like I used to think that everyone knew better than me what's good -or not good- for me, I also used to think that my partners were always right; that they had more experience, knowledge, clarity, and insights and that whatever they pointed out about me was absolutely right. And thus, if they did not see or acknowledge many of the things I mentioned in the paragraph above, it automatically meant that it was not really valuable after all.

I firmly believe that, at some point in your life, you have also based your worth on external approval. As special as I tend to think that I am, I doubt this is a "Yael" phenomenon. And so you can probably relate to the mental and emotional exhaustion linked to this, as a result of having to deal with an unpleasant and unstable self-image on a continuous basis.

I don't think I can explain where or why the shift happened in my case. I firmly believe that it was not a "one-moment" thing but the accumulation of years of work and effort to free and empower myself what eventually took me there. I was suddenly able to acknowledge my strengths; to see that my values are strongly ingrained and that I am an honorable person who chooses the seemingly hardest paths -mostly related to romantic relationships- and is willing to be responsible and to pay the costs of having chosen those paths.

Why do I say I choose the seemingly hardest paths? Because it may be easier to stay in a relationship that does not support our personal growth, in order to avoid dealing with the social and financial implications of its ending. Or because when we are generously given *most* everything, it is easier to just take it and stay. Stay, and perhaps secretly seek that little part that's missing outside of the relationship, or perhaps not seek it elsewhere but always complain about the fact that it is missing. And we would be doing this in order to avoid the possibility of losing what we have, instead of owning our actions and happiness *even at the cost of losing it all.* Furthermore, it's easier to deceitfully agree to be in a given relationship style -i.e. monogamy- and end up being with other people, than to openly state our preferences and own them *at the risk of* not finding anyone who would agree to be with us under those terms.

After all this time, I have realized that I couldn't really expect others to see me if I was incapable of seeing, acknowledging, and loving myself. And while I don't need external prizes for my honesty, transparency, and everything that I am, it is now crucial for me that the person I choose to be with is capable of *seeing* it, and does not take it for granted.

I know what it takes to be me, I know what it takes to live the unconventional life I have chosen to live, I *know* and *see* the amount of time, energy and effort I put on a daily basis to continuously become a better version of myself. I also acknowledge that I have worked hard enough to let my commitment to living in alignment with my true self be more important than the social fears and concerns that used to hold me back. Furthermore, I see that I have been willing to pay costs that are rather high to get to experience myself in the most fulfilling version possible at any given moment. Ultimately, I know, as a solid and valuable foundation, what I bring to relationships. Thus, gratefully, now I can confidently say:

> *"I know what I bring to the table... so trust me when I say that I am not afraid to eat alone".*

If you read this part and you are thinking to yourself "I really wish I can get to that point" my words to you are:

a) Spend some time alone and get to know yourself. Dedicate some time to discover what your passions are, what you truly like and don't like, what your values are, what kind of experiences you want to have in your life. Assess how much of what you are or do in your current relationships is genuine and truly satisfying, and how much of it is simply to conform to other people's ways.

b) While there is immeasurable value in identifying the ways of being or things we do in relationships that don't work, there is just as much in acknowledging all the ones that do. And don't minimize anything, every little bit counts.

c) If you are like I was, many times we question why someone would want to be with us, if we are so [fill in the blank]. But after completing parts a) and b), I invite you to turn the question around and start asking: "why would I want to be with someone who is not capable of seeing all that I am?"

d) You don't have to take my word for it, but I will put it out anyway: we will be much better off in the long run being alone, than being in a relationship in which we have to hold ourselves back or in which we are not seen.

I know this last point can be controversial. Many people may argue that it is nicer to be in a relationship, even if that means making compromises and living with things that will have to be given up. My take is that no one *should* have to change who they are or give up on what's important for them in order to be in a relationship and avoid being alone. If they were to do it, it should be because they genuinely *want to* or *see the value* in doing so, and therefore choose to. Otherwise, I believe it would only work for so long before resentment would start to creep up. I will reiterate this quote from Lisa Nichole that really speaks to this point:

"It's your responsibility to show the world how to treat you by the way in which you treat yourself"

If you show the world that it's okay to step over what's important to you in order to "gain" or "maintain" something, there's no reason why the world or other people would not step over a lot of things as well. Whereas, if you show the world that you are not going to put up with anything less than you know you deserve, it and the people will follow your example and won't deliver anything less.

BELIEF XI: I've got to prove my worth

This belief was strongly intertwined with -and negatively influenced by- some of the other ones we discussed earlier. It was not enough that I believed that I did not think I had skills, abilities or that I was worthy, but I also believed that I needed to prove something to people and that I clearly had nothing to prove it with! This could explain why, even though I attempted to dissolve this belief many years ago, it was not until some of the other ones were transformed that I was finally able to tackle this one.

A large part of the intense effect that this belief had on me stemmed from another mistaken thought which was that I had control over what other people would think, say, or do about me. I used to think that I was *that* powerful; as though if I modified or limited my actions of speech and body, I would be able to directly influence other people's perception of me. Let me give you some examples:

If I made a life-decision (i.e. to move to Israel, to get married, to get divorced, to date someone who's not Jewish like I am, to date someone who's transgender, etc.) I needed to make sure I fully justified the reasons for that decision. I couldn't just say "I chose this because I chose this", because that would have left too much room for interpretation and

45

judgment, and I used to think that I could not emotionally afford to deal with that. People needed to see that my decision was smart, well thought out, and perfectly justified, and that it was not simply a 'spur of the moment' thing. As you will discover I have made many life choices that can be considered unconventional, so this need to look good, prove myself and justify my actions was a very prominent -and exhausting- constant in my life.

I used to love social media, and in a way, I still do. However, what I use it for and where I share things from has shifted over the past few years. For a while, I used to share the most positive and exciting aspects of my life in order to get approval. If I got a lot of 'likes', it would mean that people could see that my choices (my partners, where I lived, etc.) had been the right ones, and would not think that I am too crazy after all. However, if I did not get much of a response, then it was a direct correlation with people's lack of agreement, approval, or appreciation for what I was doing and the way I was living. Clearly, according to my thought process, if none of that was present, it meant that my choices were not as great as I thought.

If I was sharing with someone about a breakthrough I had had in my life, or a personal accomplishment, I couldn't just say "this is what happened". I needed to make sure I told them all the details of what that took from me and all that I had to get through internally to achieve it because they would otherwise not realize the magnitude and think it was not such a big deal. And the same applied for when I had a breakdown. I needed to let them know why the situation was so challenging for me and why it was such a struggle because they would otherwise think I was exaggerating and making it a bigger deal than it really was.

I write this and simply laugh at the absurdity of it all. My need for approval was extreme, and so was my misconception of anything I did -or did not do- actually being able to influence people's perception of me. Don Miguel Ruiz, in his book The Four Agreements, worded it clearly in his second agreement:

"Whatever happens around you, don't take it personally. Nothing other people do is because of you. It is because of themselves. All people live in their own dream, in their own mind; they are in a completely different world from the world we live in. When we take something personally, we make the assumption that they know what is in our world, and we try to impose our world on their world… What they say, what they do, and the opinions they give are according to the agreements they have in their own minds."

My growth in this area partly came from the progressive realization that how people thought or spoke about me was completely out of my control, and was not related to my reality but rather to theirs. Furthermore, it was also greatly influenced by my disposition to inquire into the "why" I behaved the way I did in my relationships.

For instance, a couple of years ago, when I started dating a transgender man, I was having a really strong internal battle between telling my parents or close friends about him or not. Either choice was anxiety-provoking for me. I felt like if I did not tell them, then I was creating an emotional barrier and causing some distance between us. But if I told them, I was exposing myself to hearing some of those comments that I now know would just be coming from *their* reality, but that immediately would make me doubt mine.

I believed that my reason for sharing with them was *not* because that's what I wanted to do at that specific moment in my relationship, but rather because I thought that doing so was *required* if what I wanted was to be close to them.

I was able to discern and question this thinking pattern and realize that it was not necessarily so. This allowed me to start taking some time and space to figure things out on my own and *then* share them with my loved ones. My choices started being in alignment with what I genuinely wanted, and they were no longer influenced by their opinions, approval, or lack thereof.

I usually love to look for quotes that can express what I am feeling or thinking, but this was the very first time that an image spoke to me way louder than words. I found an image of five starting stalls for an animal race. Four of them had greyhounds who were already starting to run, and the fifth one had a cheetah who was lying inside the stall, simply looking outward. To me, that was a very clear statement that said: "I know I am fast, and I would beat them in a heartbeat, but I don't have a need to go out and show off or prove that to anyone".

Now I share when I am ready, and not when I feel like I *need to*. My active participation in social media has decreased significantly, and when I do it, I come from "how can what I want to share contribute to others" rather than from "the value of my share and the extent of my life's greatness depends on people's response to what I post".

It is not so much *what* we do but *where* we do it from that makes a difference. Perhaps at some point, I will find myself sharing a lot again, but there is a difference between sharing in search of validation and sharing that comes from a commitment to making a contribution.

In 2018 I did an Introduction to Buddhism silent retreat in Dharamkot, India, and one of the greatest things I got from the most basic level of Tibetan Buddhism was: if my actions are coming from a self-centered attachment to something (in this case, to external approval or validation), that is prone to lead to anger if not fulfilled -which is very likely-, then I am much better off restraining my actions *unless or until* I can come from an intention to benefit something greater than me. It requires a lot of self-awareness and self-control, but doing it certainly alters our experience of ourselves and of the world around us.

I want to wrap up this chapter with the following quote by Henry Ford:

"Whether you think you can, or you think you can't,
you are right"

It all starts with what we believe. I would not say that the moment we think we can, we will be able to because that is not necessarily the case. However, if we believe we can and we keep searching for ways to make it happen, it eventually will. It is fascinating to discover how different life can appear in two distinct moments in which the only thing that has changed is the belief. It can be that none of the outside conditions have been altered, and yet because our belief has, the world occurs in a completely new, pleasant, and promising way - or vice versa.

It is also relevant for us to be aware of the concept of *impermanence;* remembering that nothing lasts forever. Why do I bring this up? Because during the process of writing this chapter, I have gone back and forth from empowering to non-empowering beliefs multiple times. I may feel blissful in one moment realizing how differently I feel about myself and how much more competent and confident I think I am on certain topics, and then something happens that pulls the rug from under me and the opposite becomes true, and then, it doesn't anymore. I tend to wish that if I have already attained a certain level of empowerment, it would remain like that forever, you know? And then, I remind myself that everything changes, and this is no exception.

CHOOSING TO LIVE AN UNCONVENTIONAL LIFE, IN ALL THAT IT ENTAILS

Growing up, I always thought that my life would be as follows: I would graduate from High school and join an international travel program that my cousins and middle brother had been part of called Up With People, which empowers young adults to make a difference through volunteering, leadership and performing arts. After my year traveling the world, I would start university in Mexico, and eventually meet someone, get married, have kids, and work on something that I was passionate about for the rest of my life.

Little did I expect that half-way through my brother's year in Up with People, the company would go bankrupt and that part of my plan would be canceled. Now it is up and running again, but too late for me... Instead of joining this program, I went to Israel for eight months, discovered a world that I liked much better than the little bubble I used to live in Mexico, and decided to move there. I wanted to do as the Israelis did -travel the world prior to starting college and settling down- but lacked the courage to do it. Hence, the way my life unfolded afterward was not that radically different from how I initially thought it would be. I got married to a Jewish guy, I went to college, got a job, a car, a house… No kids yet, because I felt like I was still too young and not ready, but thus far my life was pretty much following the path drawn by the community I had grown up in.

Much of what I am going to say may not seem like a big deal to many of you who grew up in more open-minded, relaxed environments. But for anyone who grew up as part of a tight community like the Jewish community in Mexico, anyone who was repeatedly told what their life should and shouldn't be like, I am sure you can understand how conflicting it was for me to openly and confidently own my life events and choices.

Things started to shift when at twenty-eight years old I was already getting divorced. Nowadays it may not be so unusual, but at that time it felt like it was almost shameful to admit that a) my marriage hadn't worked out and b) that I knew the role I had played in the way it turned out.

Next was me getting married again, but this time to someone who was not Jewish. In my hometown, mixed marriages were generally frowned upon. We were supposed to marry someone who was Jewish, for the continuation of our people and traditions. I do believe that the fact that I lived in the US at that point made it more manageable for me to be with him; I am not sure how -or if- I could have handled the social and family pressure, had I lived in Mexico. But having met someone that I connected with so amazingly on so many levels, I couldn't justify ending the relationship simply because we did not share the same religious background.

This in itself is already unconventional, and it took a lot of courage and assertiveness for me to introduce him to my family and to firmly choose to move forward with our relationship despite their initial reactions. As a funny anecdote, he chose to propose to me on Christmas Day.

I was extremely excited about the proposal, but also freaking out about what people would say after asking "how did he propose?" and I would say, "well, we were opening our gifts on Christmas morning and... ". Jews having a Christmas tree at home and receiving gifts is Not something either accepted or approved of. While I was hesitant to agree to have a tiny tree at the house, even though nobody would have to have known about it, all of a sudden, I found myself exposed to everyone finding out that I had gotten engaged to someone who is not Jewish.

It turned out that my fear of people's reactions was worse than the reactions themselves; everyone seemed to have been really fond of him and welcomed him nicely into my family. We got married, got a dog, we both worked, traveled, had a pretty active social life, and were planning on getting pregnant soon... Yet, parallelly to this normalcy was the ongoing inquiry into -and discovery of- my sexual identity and relationship-style preference, of which he was aware from the very beginning, but I hadn't consolidated yet. The moment it became clear to me that I was not willing to live my life without exploring my attraction to women or suppressing my love for multiple people, my second marriage came to an end.

I was now a thirty-one-year-old woman who had gotten married and divorced twice. Talking about one divorce was uncomfortable, now imagine having two! I was certain that whoever found out would gossip about me and conclude that there must be something wrong with me, that I couldn't maintain a relationship long-term. Nevertheless, this concern did not stop me from sticking to what I thought was best for me and from moving on with my life.

At the time my second husband and I got separated, I did not have a job because he had encouraged me and supported me to leave the one I had to pursue the development of an invention I had come up with which did not pan out. Without a husband or a job, I did not have anything keeping me from leaving other than my dog Zoey. My best friend suggested I should find someone to look after Zoey and travel, which was something I had always wanted to do. I started looking into options to work abroad and ended up deciding on what was supposed to be a 2-month trip to Southeast Asia.

During that trip, I discovered yet another world that I liked even more than the ones I had experienced in Israel and in the US. Less than two weeks into the trip I was already exploring my options to stay there and work, and when it was time for me to head back, I had already arranged everything I needed in order to be able to stay. I missed my flight and started living the life I had always wanted to live.

I settled down in Vietnam. Vietnam?! Who would have ever imagined I would end up living there? I remember China always being used as a joke when implying that where someone lived was extremely far away. And now I was living in a neighboring country! I was teaching English for a living instead of working in Occupational Therapy and was riding a motorbike to work with a helmet and all the sun, dust, and rain-protection gear that Vietnamese traditionally wear. I was living in a 2-bedroom apartment that was pretty basic and outdated, next to the city's market area, instead of in my 3-bedroom beautiful lakefront house in Florida.

I was living off of a wardrobe that had such few clothes that they could almost all fit in a large suitcase, rotating between the same six dresses to go to work for a whole year and a half, instead of having a full-size walk-in closet and buying myself new clothes regularly. I was using a slow cooker and two bowls, two plates, one pan, one wok, one cutting board, one peeler, two cutting knives, one large spoon and two sets of chopsticks instead of having a fully equipped kitchen with all sorts of appliances and gadgets and an abundance of cutlery and dishes... You get the picture of how dramatic my lifestyle change was. And yet, I was the happiest I had ever been in my entire life.

Life was no longer about keeping up with a society that works to try to pay for things that we never finish paying for because there is always something else we think we need to get in order to be happy. It was no longer about doing things that I knew were good for me 'if I had the time or energy to do them' but rather about having those things be my top priority, understanding that my physical, spiritual and emotional wellbeing were the foundation for the rest of my life to work well. The level or quality of my contribution was not dependent on how well I looked or how many different outfits I had, but rather on who I was when I was with my students and how confident I was in terms of my skills and what I bring to the table.

The quality of my relationships started to shift as well. I used to only be interested in nurturing friendships with people who wanted to talk about deep, personal, and meaningful conversations and did not find value in sharing with people otherwise. And suddenly, being in a country in which I did not speak the language, I started to connect with people and develop beautifully close relationships that did not depend on the depth of our conversations. Instead, they depended on our willingness and ability to be present with each other, to make it a point to make each other feel welcomed, included and loved despite the limited communication possible, and on our openness to appreciate and enjoy each other's company.

When I first arrived in Vietnam, I signed a six-month contract to teach because I was not willing to commit to a longer period. I wanted to take it one step at a time; I did not want to feel like I was tied down or forced to stay in a place that I perhaps would not want to be in after some time. Funnily enough, I ended up extending my contract two more times, for a total of a year and a half. In a really strange way, and even though it turned out to be the same eighteen months that they originally would have wanted me to commit to, the act of breaking it down made it a lot more manageable for my recently-freed spirit.

Looking back, I can start to pinpoint that what I lacked at that time -and still struggle with to an extent- was the confidence and assertiveness to know that I am *not* bound to stay anywhere I am not happy or fulfilled. Because of my codependent traits -which included placing my worth in other people's ability to see me, agree with me, or love me, and feeling responsible for how others felt and what they dealt with as a result of my actions- I used to feel stuck and stay in places that did not work for me or that were no longer where I wanted to be. Therefore, six-months at a time

56

was a model that allowed me to still feel free to *choose* to be there. In fact, as time goes by, I am learning more and more about how creating my own *alternative models of living* makes life that much more manageable and enjoyable.

Why do I make this last statement? Because I have identified that feeling like "I have no other option" has been a source of resistance and anguish for me. For example, for a long time motherhood showed up for me that way: I was preparing to move towards it with my second husband, but it was mostly because 'not having kids' did not exist as an option for me. However, the more I have gotten to know and understand myself, the clearer it has become that, had I not questioned this at all, I would most likely have resented my kids afterward for all that I had given up for them. On a similar note, I was being monogamous, not because that was what I really wanted but because I felt like I had no option if what I wanted was to keep my partners around. Had I not challenged this model as well and stuck to it forever, I would have undoubtedly ended up resenting my partner.

In both of these examples, I mention that I would have resented others: either my kids or my partners. Unknowingly, who I would have been truly resenting was myself, not them, for having let life happen *to* me, and having become "a victim" of it, instead of owning that I could have questioned and challenged life as it was coming towards me, and I did not.

What I am trying to get to is that the actions may or may not end up being the same, but *Where* those actions are taken from would make all the difference. I may -or may not- end up being a mom, but if I am, it will have been out of choice and not because I thought that I *had* to. I may -or may not- end up in a monogamous relationship, but if I do, It will have been out of choice and not out of fear of losing my partner. I may -or may not- be in a relationship with a transgender man or with a woman instead of a man, but if I don't, it will have been because I gave things a try and they did not work out, and not because I did not dare to do it out of fear of losing approval, respect or love from people in my life. I may -or may not- one day end up moving back to where my family lives, but if I do, It will have been out of choice and not out of feeling guilt or like I am a bad family member otherwise. I may -or may not- end up settling down in a place at some point instead of intending to travel the world indefinitely, but if I do, it will be out of choice and not out of feeling like I need to meet social expectations or standards. I may -or may not- end up living a materially abundant lifestyle, but if I do, it will be out of choice and not out of feeling like I *need* to in order to prove something.

Most recently I met a wonderful woman who wanted to be in a relationship with me. Based on my past experiences, I was terrified to commit to a long-term relationship again. So, we came up with the idea of being asked to be her girlfriend *just for the day,* and she would ask that every day. Or perhaps, eventually, I would start asking her too. That way, being in a relationship would be something I (we) get to actively choose every day, and it would not be something I feel trapped or forced (by myself) to be in. This may sound ridiculous to some of you, and it may come across as a lack of commitment. But as I will further elaborate a little later, my greatest commitment is to myself, to always tell and live my truth.

My truth is that I am here, as beautifully worded by Neale Donald Walsch, and adopted as my own thought, to *"recreate myself anew, in every golden moment of Now, in the next grandest version of the greatest vision ever I held about Who I Am".*

Thus, if at some point, remaining in that -or in any other- relationship does not allow for me to fulfill my purpose, then I may choose to no longer be there. And if I were to stay, it will have been out of a conscious and deliberate choice made every day, and not out of fear, guilt, codependency, or any other unproductive reason.

I am not sure how this would translate into marriages, during which it is commonly vowed: "until death do us part". Perhaps it does not translate at all, and it means that I will never get married again. Or perhaps, it means that we get to write our own vows and create some that fit our alternative and consensual perspective on life and relationships. Yet, if the latter weren't an option -meaning that I don't find anyone whose mindset in that regard is similar to mine- then the former would be preferable over giving my word to something or someone that could potentially interfere with my life's purpose.

To sum everything up, I do not have any set life plans for the next five, ten, or even one year… I have an absolutely clear vision of what I want every area of my life to *feel* like: my health and wellbeing, my emotional life, my spiritual life, my intellectual life, my character, my love relationships, parenting (if I were to pursue it), my social life, my career, my finances, and the quality of my life. Yet, I am not attached to any of it having to *look* any particular way. And I am perfectly content living this way and learning to love and embrace uncertainty.

I am making strides towards turning this vision into a reality, and I *KNOW* that the timing and ways in which it will unfold will be absolutely perfect.

I will add here, however, that getting to the point of being comfortable living this way has not been easy, especially being someone who used to do whatever possible to keep people from talking about me. I would like to share the lessons I have learned, and how I have reached the point where I am in my life, even though I still am and will always be a work in progress.

1) People *will* talk about others. And they will most likely talk about me, no matter what I do. But they will only do so until they find something new and more exciting to give their attention to. This pattern repeats itself over and over again, and whatever they say, is never a reflection of me or whoever they are talking about, but rather of who *they* are and what they choose to spend their energy on. It is often easier to look outside to avoid dealing with what goes inside us.

2) It *is* okay for me to share whatever is going on in my life *once I am set and clear* on what direction I am heading. I used to bring up whatever I was going through with my family and friends as it happened, and as you can imagine, everyone had their own opinion as far as what I should or shouldn't do. This used to drive me crazy! Because it did not allow me to connect with what I really wanted. More than listening to myself, I was

worried about how I could handle things or move forward without disappointing anyone.

How I learned this last lesson was by distinguishing that I had equaled closeness with a need to share *everything* I was experiencing. Let me explain. I have lived away from my family since I was eighteen years old, and at some point, I came up with the idea that the only way for me to stay close to my loved ones through the distance was by telling them every-little-thing that was going on in my life. I firmly believed that, if I did not, I was actually creating a barrier between me and them. Crazy, huh? But having come up with that decision had made me feel obligated to share my processes with people, no matter how uncomfortable that was!.

This only started to change, as I shared before, when I met my former partner who was a transgender man. I was exploring the relationship with him, and simultaneously freaking out about how my parents would react once I told them that I was dating someone who is transgender. I was blessed to have the support of an old family friend who was involved in Guimel, the organization that supports the LGBTQ Jewish community in Mexico, and she told me "you don't have to tell your parents about this while you figure things out. Once you are sure that this is the direction you are taking, you can open up to them. You can always use my support if you feel you need it". It is strange because, in a way, it felt like she was giving me permission to keep certain things to myself that I never knew or thought I should. It was a wonderful gift I got from her. Going forward, I was no longer impulsively sharing with people just to maintain closeness. This had a tremendous impact on my overall emotional state.

3) Nobody knows better than we do what is best for us. People will have many opinions and suggestions of what they think we should or should not do, but *none* of them will actually have to deal with the consequences of following their advice.

I can't recall the exact details of how this conversation went, but I believe it took place around the time when I was considering moving to Israel. A friend of mine told me something like: "you should not move to Israel and be away from your family" and I thought to myself: "If I don't move, will she make sure that I am happy and fulfilled here? Of course not. She will live her life and how I feel by staying here will not be her responsibility".

Fast forward 17 years. I live in Vietnam and my family often tells me how much they miss me and they would love to have me close. I miss them too and would love to be physically close to them too. However, if I lived in Mexico, I would see them twice, maybe three times a week. What about the quality of my life for the rest of the time? They may not mind dealing with the traffic as much as I do; they wouldn't have to potentially take a job that they don't enjoy, or even if I enjoyed it, that would barely make ends meet and would bring back the financial stress I have worked so hard to get rid of. They wouldn't switch from working twenty-two hours a week to working forty or more plus dealing with the commute, having significantly less time to work on the things that are important to them on a personal level... For some, being close to their family is worth paying all of the above costs and more. For me, my wellbeing and the quality of my everyday life are way more important than being able to physically spend time with them a few hours a week. I am grateful for the technology that in many ways bridges the gap between the countries. Furthermore, the more I take care of me, the better place I am in to be FOR them and with them when I do see them. Might this change at some point? Perhaps. But right now, knowing that no one other than me is responsible for my wellbeing, I choose the life that I know works best for me, even if it means being physically away from them.

4) Nothing is guaranteed in life, other than change and death. There is no way for us to know with absolute certainty that something is going to turn out exactly the way we want it or intend it to. Thus, I much rather give things a try and live with "oh well", than out of fear of stepping into the unknown or out of my comfort zone always wonder "what if".

As you can tell from my life story, most of the things have not turned out the way I expected. After one divorce, some people may be too hesitant to enter into a relationship again. I was too, but decided to give myself the chance to try again, and then again after the second divorce, and then again after my last long-term open and committed relationship. Opening myself up once more is emotionally challenging, but you never know what blessings and/or lessons may come from every new opportunity that shows up.

After one unsuccessful business or project initiative, some people may not want to give it another shot and prefer to stay in safe, familiar grounds. I have been discouraged for sure, but I have also kept on trying and will continue to do so until something takes off.

When I have an idea of what my possible next plan is, something tends to happen that challenges it. When this occurs, I don't insist on sticking to the original plan. Instead, I flow with things and see where life takes me. I will give you an example: the past couple of months I had been working on unlocking my brain capacity and developing teaching methods that could enhance my students' language acquisition skills alongside their overall ability to learn. I was very excited to present this to the English Center I work for and to work with them to find ways to make it available not only to my own students but to everyone who studies at the center.

Immediately after I introduced this to the head of the school, the coronavirus started to spread and schools closed in Vietnam. It has been over four months since then. While my proposal might have been a great asset for the company, the chances of it being pursued anytime soon - due to the financial impact that the pandemic is having on everyone- are very slim.

I don't know if I will drop it altogether. For now, I have switched gears and am focusing all my energy on making this book a reality. Which one of these projects will take off? I don't know. It may be the book, it may be the educational project, it may be both or it may be something new and totally different. But I am giving everything a try, knowing that what's in the largest amount of people's best interest is what will come to life.

5) There is no right or wrong way of living, and there is no "one size fits all" either. There is no way in which we are "supposed to" live because anything and everything that

happens is an opportunity for growth. We may find that a choice we made was not the most beneficial for the purpose we intended, but it nevertheless brought about a lesson that can enhance the quality of our lives and relationships in the future. Or we may find that our choice resulted in beautiful and extraordinary progress towards fulfilling our purpose to be the best version of ourselves.

Have you ever given yourself the chance to question why you are doing what you are doing? Is the life you are living now the one you absolutely love, have always dreamed of, and would choose over and over again? Or are there aspects of it that you are simply living by default, or out of fear of making changes because you can't predict how things will turn out? There is nothing right or wrong about living one way or the other. However, there is a magnificent level of inner-freedom and fulfillment when we can confidently say that every aspect of our lives is in 100% alignment with Who We Really Are.

OPENING UP AND BEING WILLING TO STEP INTO THE UNKNOWN

Life is unpredictable, we never know what's going to happen next. Yet, there is a certain level of predictability that can be attained when you live a more traditional life. For instance, if you are employed at a company, you can pretty confidently anticipate the tasks that you will have to do the next day; you know you can expect that on payday you will receive your paycheck, and you can make plans because you have a general idea of what you schedule is like on a regular basis.

You also probably have a set routine. You know that on Mondays after work you meet up with your friends, on Tuesdays and Thursdays you have your tennis practice, and Friday evenings you have dinner with your family. If you are someone who likes to go to the gym every morning, you already know more or less the amount of traffic you will hit at the time you normally go, and how busy the gym will be. You know at what time you will need to leave your house to make it to work on time, and that, if it is Monday, there will most likely be a box of freshly baked donuts next to the coffee machine at the office.

Obviously, there can always be unexpected events that will alter this familiarity, but overall, you pretty much know what's coming.

This starts to change, for example, when you choose to be an entrepreneur for the first time, and even more in an area that you are not familiar with. You don't really have a set schedule (unless you have created it yourself to have some sort of structure, or you have certain meetings to attend) and you know what you are up to, but you don't really know everything that this new venture is going to entail. You may find that, on the go, you start realizing information or skills that you needed to have that you were not aware of, and you have to figure out a way to learn them, or you may think that you will close a deal and have money in your pocket by a specific date but it does not turn out as you expected. Entrepreneurship is certainly an arena that requires you to step into the unknown, and for those of you who have pursued this at some point, you know that this is not always a comfortable state to be in.

I, particularly, did not use to enjoy such a state. I liked having a sense of security of what was going to happen and when; that I had everything I could require to make sure that whatever was needed would be taken care of, and I basically wanted to know the outcome -and know that it would be a positive one- because the fear of failure felt terrifying.

Then, I started traveling. But there is traveling and *traveling*. There are those who have everything perfectly planned and arranged for months in advance; they know exactly where they are going to be, when and for how long they will be there, where they are going to stay and what they are going to do during their visit. They read books and blogs about the place they will visit and make sure they have as much information as possible, to feel confident that the trip will turn out perfectly -or as perfect as possible.

And then, there is me. On my first solo trip, I knew that I was going to travel for two months, that I wanted to visit four countries, and that I was flying into Thailand. I knew where I would stay in Bangkok; I was going to stay with a member of Servas, a worldwide non-profit organization that aims to create world peace and understanding through a network of hosts and travelers who participate in cultural exchanges. But I did not know exactly for how long I would stay at his place, nor did I have the slightest idea of where I was going to go next.

I was very fortunate to have been hosted by an amazing man who immediately immersed me into the culture, who took me to markets and introduced me to all sorts of foods that I would have never tried on my own, and who somehow gave me the confidence to start exploring by myself. During the first week, I met up with a couple of other members of this organization, who also encouraged my spirit of adventure. And from that moment on, all I did was *flow.*

My initial trip was supposed to include Thailand, Laos, Cambodia, and Vietnam. I spent two weeks in Thailand, two in Laos, the rest in Vietnam, and I did not leave. There are endless amazing stories that I could share about each of the places I visited, the people I met, how my plans came about, how much my plans changed from one moment to the next, how many times I got lost, or ended up being in hostels or places that provided me with many anecdotes to tell. It was all spontaneous, it was all adventurous, and it was the best experience of my life.

Quite often, I faced uncertainty during the trip. I was not sure that the choices I was making -as far as my next destination or step to take- were the best ones, and also, most of the time, I did not know what to expect next. Yet, I was the calmest and most peaceful I had ever been. I stopped worrying about "getting it right" and started trusting life and looking at everything that happened -especially the breakdowns and mess-ups- as opportunities to learn something, and as wonderful, entertaining stories to tell.

I'm going to give you an example of something that happened a few years later, but that clearly portrays what I am trying to say. My brother and sister-in-law were going to get married in Israel, and I did not think I was going to go but at the last minute decided it was not something I wanted to miss. I managed to arrange for all my classes to be covered in Vietnam and booked my flight, but because it was with such short notice, I could not take too many days off. Here are two versions of what happened:

Version 1 - I flew to Israel, was able to surprise my brother and his new wife and, even though my visit was brief, I got to share in that special moment with my whole family, Then, I flew back to Vietnam. Everything went smoothly, all the flights ran on time. It was a beautiful trip.

Version 2 - I flew to Israel, barely spent forty-eight hours there, and between the adrenaline of having shown up as a surprise to them and the number of events to attend in such a short period of time, I hardly got any sleep. I was exhausted. I made it back to the airport and had my connecting-flight ticket printed from Israel, so once I got to Moscow I went to the designated gate. I saw that the departure time was getting closer and no signs of my flight were there, so I realized I was at the wrong gate. I ran to the 'correct' one and saw a bunch of people standing in line, so I relaxed and waited next to them.

Minutes kept passing by and it was almost time for my flight to leave. I freaked out and finally asked people where they were flying to and when they answered "Shanghai" I realized I had gotten the signs and lines confused. I ran to the actual gate and the attendants told me "the gates are closed, you have been in the airport for more than three hours, there is no reason for you to have been this late, I am sorry". I went to the counter and found out that they only have one flight per day, and that the next flight was at the same time the following day.

Just so you know, as an American, you need to have a visa to enter Russia. I clearly did not have one, since I was just supposed to be there in transit. I was wrapping my mind around spending the next twenty-four hours at the airport as Tom Hanks did in The Terminal, but I called a Russian friend in Vietnam, and he mentioned that Israelis don't need a visa to enter. Thankfully, I was able to use my Israeli documents and enter the country.

I have many more really cool stories to share about what happened once I was in Moscow, of how difficult it was to get around late at night in a country where most people don't speak English and I had no battery left on my phone, and how once I managed to get to the hostel my friend had booked for me, the only other person that was there and spoke English also spoke Spanish because he happened to be Mexican… But I think by now you get the point.

In this story, the *known* would have been for me to say "I don't have the money to make this trip and I did not give my employer enough notice to find coverage, so I will stay and continue to go to work as scheduled". The *unknown* was to say "this is not something I want to miss, I don't know how I will make it happen financially and logistically speaking, but I will give it a try", and the rest is history.

Which one of the stories is more enticing? I don't know about you, but I, hands down, prefer the second one. Having missed my flight could have been a ridiculous source of stress and anxiety, but for some reason, during my first trip, I had developed the ability to embrace and enjoy these mishaps.

I have truly been impressed by my ability to laugh at all of these situations during my travels and to not stress out about them *knowing* that everything always turns out just fine and that, no matter where I am, I am always going to be taken care of.

I have made it a point to do my best to transfer such *knowledge* into my everyday life, but for some reason, outside of the context of traveling, it has continued to be a challenge. Nevertheless, the lessons learned during my travels have been extraordinarily useful in supporting and empowering me to *dare* to step into the unknown.

I often face a struggle between my rational mind and my emotional one. The emotional side still manages to worry, despite the rational side knowing that what my trips have shown me, life has shown me as well.

There has been no time in which I encountered a challenge -no matter how difficult it was- and things didn't eventually work out or fall into place. I am still alive, those problems have brought about growth and experience, and I am grateful to be able to live a fulfilling life. And I have always encountered amazing people along the way that have supported me in making it happen. Thus, despite the worry, I always go for it.

I dare to assert that, if you look back at your life, you will find that it has been the exact same case. Things that were unknown and that seemed scary or worrisome came and went, and you have come out of them stronger and with many lessons learned.

Gratitude is one of the greatest values I have developed, and I would say that it is the most important one to own when facing life in general, but mostly when facing the unknown.

If things turn out as planned -just as if I had I been able to get on my original return flight to Vietnam- we can be grateful that everything went smoothly and seamlessly. If things don't turn out as planned -like in this situation, where I missed my flight- we can be grateful for the lessons learned. In this case, I learned to double-check my gate as soon as I get to the next airport, that family celebrations are blessings, and that no extra savings can replace the joy of sharing with them, among other things.

Magic does not happen in familiar and predictable grounds. Life can be great, and we can be happy and content if we stay there, I have no doubt about it. However, there is a whole other level of fulfillment that becomes available when we are willing to step into the unknown and we have the opportunity to discover whole new worlds that we would not have known had we stayed in the safe zone.

LEARNING TO LISTEN TO OUR BODIES

"Your body is your best guide. It constantly tells you, in the form of pain or sensations, what's working for you and what's not"
- Hina Hashimi, **Your Life: A Practical Guide to Happiness, Peace, and Fulfilment**

If we set off from the idea that we are born without a manual -one that tells us how to effortlessly navigate through life, how to relate to ourselves and others in a healthy way, and how to optimally use our minds and bodies- it is understandable that we will encounter quite a few breakdowns in the process of figuring it all out. No doubt about it, this has been the case for me, but I have slowly been discovering that our bodies, when we learn to listen to them, have a much greater function than the one I originally thought of simply being the "suit" in which we live, the one that allows us to get around and experience life in the physical plane.

As the years have gone by, and I have dealt with and overcome a few different medical conditions, I have realized that my body has always been "speaking" to me, letting me know whether something I am doing is working for me or it is not. Yet, for a very long time, I did not know I should listen nor how to listen to it.

.

Let me explain what I mean with this example: there were certain foods I used to eat that would make me feel either bloated or sluggish after I ate them. I would get a hunch that perhaps I was feeling that way because of what I had eaten, and I would stop eating these items for a period of time. Temporarily removing them from my diet would make me feel significantly better, but soon after that, my desire for immediate gratification -because they tasted *so* good- would take over, and I would start eating them again. As you can imagine, this did not do for good results.

The same thing happened in the area of exercise. I would feel lethargic, stiff, and uncomfortable in my own body, so I would push myself to participate in some sort of physical activity. I would do so for a couple of days -or during my lucky times, a couple of weeks- and I would feel much more energized, and light. All of a sudden, one morning, staying in bed would seem appealing, and I would allow my immediate satisfaction -relaxing for a little longer- to take control. Thus I would skip my workout for one day, and then another day, and the next thing I knew I had stopped exercising altogether and was feeling lousy all over again.

I don't think I needed doctors to tell me what things to stop eating in order to feel better; I was clear on what those were. I also did not need them to tell me to exercise regularly; I already knew that too. I simply wasn't willing to make -or commit to- the changes that my body had been suggesting on its own. Either my awareness at the time did not support *feeling good* as my top priority yet, or I was resisting it for whatever reason, but I was certainly ignoring straightforward courses of action I could take.

Our bodies may not speak to us through words, but they certainly do so through the way we feel. Our level of awareness and our commitment to our well-being marks the amount of attention we actually pay to our body's communication. This happens for two main reasons:

1) Perhaps we have a commitment to feeling well but have not yet developed the capacity to distinguish what or how what we do -or don't do- affects us, in which case it's just a matter of slowing down and *starting to pay attention.*

2) Perhaps we do have that ability to discern, but we have a greater commitment to feeling unconstrained and free to do what we want when we want it than to feel good, in which case being able to listen to the body's communication makes no difference at all.

In the two examples related to food and exercise, I belonged to the second category. A dear friend of mine, Brandy, who passed away a couple of years ago, used to tell me:

"You are always winning the game you are playing"

What this quote tells me is that we are not always honest with ourselves about what game we are playing. In my case, I used to complain about feeling poorly -and make it seem like I was losing at the game of feeling well-, but I was failing to acknowledge that I was actually playing "I don't want to limit or force myself", and I was certainly victorious. It was not until my commitment -or the game I chose to play- shifted, that I was able to make the switch to actually listen to the way my body felt and act accordingly.

In comparison, there were other situations in which I responded a little faster. For example, I have had four surgeries on my right hand that, with so much invasion to the same area, left it quite sensitive. Right after my last surgery, I started experiencing very severe pain that I realized intensified even further with the use of my cell phone. The doctor never told me "you should not use your phone too much" or "you should adapt it in some way so that the stress it puts in your hands is diminished". Yet, in paying attention to how I felt during specific activities, I was able to start making modifications and noticeably decrease the pain.

I had to try to limit the amount of time I spent on my phone. Also, I modified the case to make it more ergonomic, identifying and avoiding certain sitting or lying positions that worsened the pain, but most importantly, not ignoring that the pain was there. There was a lot of trial and error of methods that could potentially help, many of them self-guided. But what was motivating me was a desire to feel well, and an unwillingness to settle for anything less.

Unlike in this last example, my readiness to do what it takes to feel good in the emotional realm took a lot longer. After more than ten years of experiencing clinical depressive episodes on and off, I finally realized that the earlier symptoms of my condition were nothing but warnings that my body was sending to let me know that the route I was taking was *not* the one I needed to take.

Fairly recently, I learned about a term in psychology known as *cognitive dissonance,* which refers to a lack of consistency between what we think or believe, and what we do. What I realized, after thinking back to the most severe episodes I went through, is that there was a consistent and radical incongruence between what I believed was important to me and the life-choices I was making.

In the decision-making process, I could always feel the internal pull between what felt good and what I thought would be most widely approved of by my family or community/society. What led to each one of my episodes was that, out of all sorts of fears, I decided to go with the latter. My body had a way of letting me know that this was *not* what was best for me by having me experience severe anxiety and having me cry uncontrollably day after day. The accumulation of these difficult days resulted in a biochemical imbalance that, at that point, I was no longer able to get out of without the need for medication.

I would not say that my depression was merely caused by a lack of consistency between what I wanted to do and what I was actually doing. Had there not been perhaps a genetic predisposition, the consequences of this dissonance would potentially not have been as severe. However, as I have grown through experiences, developed myself more, and become more self-aware of the patterns that have repeated themselves in my life over and over again, I can confidently say that my body has given me -and continues to give me- signs when what I am about to do is not in alignment with Who I Am.

Thus, the next time an emotional breakdown starts to emerge, I know that the first question I need to ask myself is

"Where am I out of alignment?"

The bottom line here is that, in my journey of self-discovery, I have found that my body is a wonderful ally in living a life that is as pleasurable and fulfilling as possible. And if you are willing to see it as such, so is yours.

DISCOVERING -AND COMING TO TERMS WITH- OUR REAL SEXUAL ORIENTATION AND RELATIONSHIP-STYLE PREFERENCE

"Sexuality is the great field of battle between biology and society"
- Nancy Friday

Sexuality inevitably encompasses a large part of any person's life, and the degree and freedom with which it is explored and experienced by each individual is highly influenced by the society in which they live.

I grew up in the Jewish community in Mexico which, like many other close-knit small communities around the world, had a very traditional and fairly well-established standard of what is expected and accepted in terms of sexual identity, orientation, relationship status or relationship-style preference. And anything that did not fit those standards was criticized, condemned, and gossiped about. Everyone was expected to be attracted to a person of the opposite gender; to identify with the biological gender they were born with; to be conservative in their sexual expression, and perhaps ideally, to wait until marriage

81

before losing their virginity. People who explored and embraced their sexuality from a young age or with multiple partners were considered whores; those who were attracted to people from the same gender were pointed out and almost shamed. Individuals living together without being married were harshly judged, and the possibility of having multiple partners was inconceivable.

Because of the environment I grew up in and having learned that anything other than heterosexuality would be looked down upon and gossiped about, even the possibility of exploring the idea of having a different sexual orientation never even crossed my mind. Besides that, I happened to have a pretty easy and natural way to connect with men, with a playful and somewhat flirtatious personality, that not only makes them feel at ease and accepted, but also makes them comfortable to share and open up to me, in ways that they may not necessarily feel at ease doing with many other individuals. Hence, during my teenage years, I developed a fair amount of close friendships with men, and I often found it easier to spend time -and be myself- with them than with girls. So I simply *assumed* that my future would be with a man and in a monogamous relationship.

I went through my first marriage and divorce. By the time I started dating the man who became my second husband, I had already done a fair amount of reflection and inquiry into things that could make a difference for my future relationships. One of them was that of having the possibility to openly talk to each other if there ever was someone in our lives towards whom we felt an attraction. That way, it could be discussed and potentially consented, so if anything were ever to happen it would not have to be behind each other's back. This was partly based on what I am about to elaborate on, and also largely on knowing the enormous number of marriages worldwide in which infidelity occurs.

One of the factors that contributed to the end of my first marriage was not feeling like there was freedom to be open about any desire that would differ from the traditional monogamous model we both knew. All the challenges we were facing in our sexual intimacy -I was experiencing chronic pain with intercourse, which led to a decreased libido-, and also knowing that he still had sexual needs that I was unable to meet, I suggested for him to fulfill that part elsewhere, as long as he would be safe and tell me about it. That way, he would not constantly feel sexually frustrated, and we could continue enjoying all the other aspects of our marriage.

I know this sounds crazy and a recipe for disaster for most of you, but despite his love and patience, I felt like it was the least I could do for him; I didn't think it was fair for him to have to suffer because of my limitations. I genuinely thought this was something that could work to keep our marriage going. What happened at the end is not important, what's relevant here is to give you a background of how I started shifting towards considering having open consensual relationships.

When I first started seeing the one who became my second husband, I had this conversation with him. His first reaction was an absolute *no* to being in such a relationship; he said that If I were to bring up an attraction or desire to be with someone else, he would just leave. Nevertheless, we continued going out and developing our relationship, and the conversation progressed over time. It moved from a 'no' to a 'not now, maybe later', to a 'not with men but yes with women'. He used to bring women up and I would always wonder "why would he mention women if I am not even interested in them?". Little did I know...

A couple of years after that initial conversation, I had one of the most vivid dreams I have ever had. It was about me being at my old house, getting ready for a party with a friend who in real life is lesbian: in that scene, I was unable to control my sexual attraction towards her, so I approached her impulsively to make out with her. I woke up completely startled and confused. What had that been all about? I bravely shared my dream with this friend the following day. She listened to me graciously and then suggested I contact the sex therapist that had supported her during her 'realization' of being lesbian. I did.

After my initial session in which I shared my sexual history, I was certain the therapist would confirm that I was bisexual. Instead, she brought up the term "sexual fluidity" and recommended we attend a Tantric couples retreat that she was hosting the following weekend.

We joined the retreat, and in it, we learned a few wonderful elements that transformed the way my husband and I connected intimately, for which I was grateful. Furthermore, it provided us with a safe space to openly discuss with other couples our deepest fears and desires in terms of sexuality. It was during one of those conversations that I, for the first time ever, dared to accept that I was interested in being intimate with women as well.

The following week I was going to go on a trip where the friend I had dreamt of would also be going. Before the Tantric retreat, I had asked my husband whether he would be comfortable if I were to connect with her intimately. He said: "Let's wait and see what happens at the retreat and then I'll decide". With that in the background, one of the questions we were asked during the retreat was: "What are you afraid of?" and I said: "I'm afraid of one of these three situations: 1) my husband saying that he doesn't want me to be with this friend, because I feel like I would resent him, 2) my husband saying "go ahead" but my friend saying that she is not interested, because I would feel rejected, and 3) my husband saying "go ahead", my friend saying "let's do it" and then me actually having to do it, because I had never done it before and I was not sure what it would be like. The question was followed by "Which option would you truly want?" and I said: "I would like the third one; I would like to have my husband's consent to have the opportunity to experience being with another woman." That was such a breakthrough moment in my life! And I felt like a huge weight had been lifted off my shoulders; like I no longer had to pretend -even to myself- otherwise.

Situation number two was the one that ended up happening. My husband said okay. I had a conversation with my friend asking her if her relationship was monogamous and she said yes, and it also turned out that I had misunderstood a verbal exchange we had had the week before, in which I thought she had said that if she weren't in a relationship she would like to date me, and what she had actually said was that she would like to date someone *like* me, not me. In a way, she was 'rejecting' me as I had feared. Surprisingly, I was not upset about it; I understood how, in my desire to connect, I had heard what I wanted to hear in her words. Furthermore, whether I would have gotten to be with her or not, I was excited because I had been able to discover something about me that was life-altering.

A few weeks later, I was spending time with a group of very self-expressed, feminine, confident, and sensual women. We were talking about many things, including sex and open relationships. In one of our crazy interactions, quite randomly, one of them offered a kiss, and I impulsively took it. Despite it lasting less than two seconds, it was one of the most liberating and exhilarating moments of my life. It was the first time I had ever been able to put aside all my concerns of what other people would think or say if I did something I *truly* wanted to do, and I loved it! At that moment I knew that I would not be able to live the rest of my life without the opportunity to further explore this side of my sexual preference.

My agreement with my husband was that I would not do anything without his consent, and I honored that for the length of our relationship and up until that moment. However, that action was a spur of the moment, so I did not consult with him first. That same evening, I confessed what I had done, and I apologized for it. I had the hope that, because I did not hide what I had done even for one day, and because he knew this was important to me considering we had been having conversations about it for so long, he would forgive me and be willing to work things out to create a relationship that was fulfilling for both of us. However, that was not the case. Instead, this incident was what led to my second divorce.

It was very difficult for me to let go of what otherwise was an amazing marriage. Yet, my alternative was to commit to monogamy and heterosexuality and give up on what I had discovered about myself, suppressing a side of me that, if not expressed, in the long run, would only have led to resentment.

I chose to view my second divorce as an opportunity to get to know myself at a much deeper level. I had tapped into a side of me that I had not dared to explore before - because of all my social concerns, in addition to the fact that I had gotten married at a very young age- and now was the time to dig deeper. It felt as if I had been given a new chance to experiment and learn about myself; about my likes and dislikes, priorities, deal-breakers, and values, in a way that I had never *allowed* myself before. It felt almost as if I was living my adolescent years ten years later. I chose to no longer let my concerns about what other people would think/say dictate my behavior, and I also was -for the first time- willing to pay the price for the life I truly wanted.

I was not looking for a new, committed, long-term relationship; I knew I wasn't ready for that then. However, I was looking to meet and connect with a variety of people, while having an unwavering commitment to be fully straightforward and transparent with them about my priorities and intentions. They would know that I was bisexual and that I was interested in exploring *polyamory*, which is the practice of being able to love and be emotionally and/or sexually intimate with more than one partner, in a consensual, ethical, and responsible way.

Part of the things that I had shed light on during my quest of self-discovery was my infinite capacity to love, in addition to the beautiful vulnerability and profound connection that becomes available when topics such as emotional/sexual/sensual/romantic intimacy are explored, both in speaking and in creating such environments with others.

Even as I am writing this, it is challenging for me to feel comfortable with being open about this perspective, because I have been conditioned to believe that it is not something that is socially acceptable or appropriate to be discussed publicly. Furthermore, some people don't consider what I have defined as my motivation to be real, and they tend to assert that those elements are used to cover up not-so-pretty reasons such as fear of abandonment or rejection.

Now, a little over a year after I wrote the last paragraph, I am significantly more at peace with my relationship-style preference. But it is not so much because of the possibility to *be* with more people, rather because of what it *represents* for the people that have chosen to be in such a relationship with me. Being in [a] healthy, polyamorous relationship(s), to me, represents that my partner(s) and I are committed to experiencing a love that is *unlimited*, *eternal*, and *free*. I will elaborate on this further:

For many years, since I started the exploration of polyamory as a lifestyle, I knew that there was something about it that suits the most authentic expression of my being. And a part of me has also since believed that this is at the core of all of us, as human beings, but that most of us carry too much social weight to even allow ourselves to accept our curiosity to explore this as our possible reality. Why? Because it is not what we have been taught, it is not what we have seen, it is not the norm, it is too... liberal? And it is often misperceived or misunderstood.

Polyamory is not about having sex with anyone or everyone; it is not a "great way to justify" cheating on your partner, it is not about sex being the center of your life and relationships. It is also not even *needing* to have more than one partner, or about not wanting to commit, or about having many options in case you have a fight with someone to be able to have fun with someone else. I was never able to point out -or put into words- what it IS for me as nicely as Neale Donald Walsch did in his book Conversations with God:

"In the human reality, you will find that you always seek to love and to be loved. You will find that you will always yearn for that love to be unlimited. And you will find that you will always wish you could be free to express it. You will seek freedom, unlimitedness, and eternality in every experience of love. You may not always get it, but that is what you will seek. You will seek this because this is what love IS, and at some deep place you know that, because you ARE love, and through the expression of love you are seeking to know and to experience Who and What you are.

I would like to share how I understand each of these three words: freedom, unlimitedness, and eternality.

Unlimitedness: There is not a set amount of love that I have, that I am, or that is in me. I have the capacity to profoundly love an infinite amount of people, none of which takes an ounce of the love I give to one person away from that which I give to anyone else. In our society, a common belief is "if you are attracted to -or worse yet, love- someone else, and you are married or in a relationship, that must mean that you don't *really* love your current partner because if you did, you couldn't/wouldn't develop feelings for anyone else".

Is this the case? Does it mean that, if you have a friend and you meet someone else with whom you have a great deal of affinity and many things in common, and you become their friend as well, does that mean that your first friend wasn't 'enough' or that they weren't that important to you because if it were you wouldn't have gotten another one? If you have a second child, do you stop loving the first one -or love them a little less- because now there is someone else around? If you have a favorite shirt, and you buy another one that you really like too, does that mean that you like the first one any less? If you have a passion, let's say for reading, and all of a sudden you discover that you also thoroughly enjoy playing piano, does that make you like reading any less? Some of you might argue that none of these examples are suitable, because a love relationship is different; because you wouldn't build a life or create a family with one hundred people, while you could potentially have one hundred friends. However, this brings me to something that I want to point out, in terms of how we tend to limit our perspective by looking at the *conditions*, rather than the *principles*.

In the examples above, it is obvious that the conditions are different. But the principle is the same: we have enough love in us to appreciate and to give to an infinite number of friends, hobbies, kids, clothes, and even partners… Our TIME, however, is not unlimited, which is where the awareness comes in to say: "I cannot realistically dedicate my time to fifty partners, while also raising a family and having a career, because I wouldn't be nurturing any one of them the way I am committed to cultivating my relationships". So this is where we *choose* how we want to invest our time and how -or with whom- we want to build our lives, which leads to the second value: **Freedom**.

Another quote from Neale Donald Walsch's book says:

"If you see your decision to express your love in a particular way with only one particular other as a sacred promise, never to be broken, the day may come when you will experience that promise as an obligation - and you will resent it. Yet if you see this decision, not as a promise, made only once, but as a free choice, made over and over, that day of resentment will never come. Remember this: there is only one sacred promise- and that is to tell and live your truth". All other promises are forfeitures of freedom, and that can never be sacred. For Freedom is Who You Are".

There are a few things that I would like to address regarding this quote: It talks about expressing your love with only one person in a particular way. Ultimately, that is the *only* way we can express our love, for "love is a unique response to that which is unique", and each person is unique. So, even if we wanted to, it is impossible to love two people the exact same way. In addition, expressions do not necessarily need to be physical.

Now, there are similar *behaviors* we can use to express our love, such as holding hands, hugging, kissing, saying I love you, cuddling, having sex, talking often, and so on, which are the ones that are commonly linked with that sacred promise, also known as marriage or committed relationship. But I want you to consider the following: who has established that those are the "measurements" for a commitment? It was made up by someone, or by a group of people, who knows how long ago, and it has remained an unquestioned belief that people have been conditioned to live by. Yet, just like that was made up, each of us can 'make up' criteria or a definition that works better for us as to what being committed means.

As Steve Jobs said: *"life can be much broader once you discover one simple fact: Everything around you that you call life was made up by people that were no smarter than you. And you can change it, you can influence it... Once you learn that, you'll never be the same again."*

From my perspective, as long as there is **consensus, transparency, responsibility,** and **respect** between all parts that could be directly or indirectly impacted by the behaviors mentioned before, demonstrating -or not demonstrating- those behaviors is <u>not</u> an absolute representation of commitment or lack thereof. In fact, the values I just mentioned above, are. And while these are so for me, they may not be so for you, in which case You can create your own, for commitment or for anything else for that matter... Isn't that awesome? What's crucial, however, is that our understanding of commitment coincides with that of our partner(s).

Going back to the quote: whether it is that we commit to expressing our love through those behaviors with only one person, or we open ourselves up to the possibility of doing so with more than one person, I believe there is power in seeing it not as a promise made once, but as a free choice that we get to make over and over again, or that at some point we may no longer choose. It took me two divorces and ending one long-ish committed relationship to own the following:

The only sacred promise is to tell and live our truth.

My truth has been, is, and always will be, that I LOVE these three extraordinary beings that I shared large parts of my life with, and also, that my life's purpose is *to continue to create the next grandest version of the greatest vision I have ever held of Who I Am*, which leads up to the third quality of love that I aim to experience: **Eternality**.

In a perfect world, when I got married the first time, I would have stayed married until death does us part. Ideally, that would also have been the case with my second husband. Considering that did not happen with either one of them, I would have loved for that to have been the case with my third partner. However, and as we will all sooner or later discover in our lives, the only thing in life that is constant is change. I changed during our relationships; I progressively discovered more and more things about Who I AM which I was not able to see before, and those things I discovered were bringing me to the next grandest version of the greatest vision of Who I Am.

I am not stating this as the truth, but my experience was that there was a lack of willingness on their part to find a way to connect with the next grandest version of me; and so, ignoring what I had discovered or putting it aside just to keep these people in my life, would have been a disservice to myself because I would not have been living my truth.

You may wonder, how does this relate to eternality? First of all, in the fact that the love I have for them has never changed and never will. Even if neither one of them is physically in my life anymore, in any capacity, I will always love them infinitely. In terms of my future relationships, I don't like to consider the end of a relationship <u>as it existed</u> to be a break-up, but rather a *transition*, a transition to a different phase. In an ever-changing world and being ever-changing beings, it is very possible that, at some point, our interests and needs inside of our personal journey to become the next grandest version of Who We Are may not perfectly coincide with those of the people we are currently in a relationship with - which was clearly the case in all three relationships mentioned above. However, I firmly believe that our relationship can transition into one that supports each other in our journey, without having to cut each other off completely.

For instance, perhaps our sexual needs have changed, so we stop being sexually intimate, but the quality of our conversations was mutually enriching and empowering, and we can maintain a relationship from there. Or perhaps our spiritual needs have changed, and one of us wants to make a radical lifestyle change that the other one doesn't, so we may choose to no longer live together but to still be emotionally and sexually intimate when we do spend time together. There are no rules as far as what the new phase may look like; we get to create something that works for us.

It is funny to be writing this because I realize that, the mere definition of the term "life-partner" can be recreated so that it not only has to mean one, two, or even ten. Let me explain: In my crazy, out-there perspective of life, the fact that I am no longer married to my exes doesn't have to mean that we cannot continue to be life-partners. If there was a willingness on their part to also remain in each other's life, we could still be life-partners just not in the same capacity. We may not be the person that we live with, that we build a family with, that we see regularly. But we may nevertheless be a person that stays present in the other's life, with whom we can share our joy, growth, struggles, and everything that comes with being alive.

I have not been blessed with such quality of love yet, because my ex-partners' visions did not align with mine. But I am certain that it is possible to eternally experience and express love with more than one life-partner, even if the behaviors through which it is expressed may change. Having such a clear vision of what it is I am looking for in my next relationship -as well as Why- will allow me not to settle for anything less than I know I deserve, and than I know is possible.

As a quick side note, I want to share that redefining specific terms in a way that "feels right" to me has been an extraordinary exercise that has brought me a lot of peace in areas that I used to struggle with. You have already been exposed to my created definitions of what commitment and life-partner are. Similarly, I have redefined what it is to be in love and to be present in someone else's life, amongst other things. And every time I come up with my own definition for something, I've felt more empowered and liberated around that topic.

For instance, as I have already expressed before, I know I am someone who has an infinite capacity to love. And a few years ago, I realized that I also have the capacity to be IN LOVE with an infinite amount of people, yet not by the common definition of being in love. This whole inquiry came about after having met a girl who said she was madly in love with someone who lived in a different country, and that she was willing to leave behind the life she had built for herself in Vietnam, to be with this girl. After talking to her, I thought about how I had extremely strong feelings for someone, but it was *very* clear to me that our lifestyles were not compatible, and so I would not give up on what I had as my life vision, to take on a lifestyle that was not in alignment with it. So, I went on to ask myself: If I am unwilling to leave everything behind to be with that person, does that necessarily mean that I am not *really* in love with him or her? In other words, is that willingness -or lack of thereof- a defining factor to determine whether you are in love with someone or not?

Going by the common definition of it, most people would argue that it is a prime factor. However, according to mine, it is not. For me, being in love is:

*Being in **awe** of the real, imperfect, flawed, quirky, weird, beautiful, and magical being that someone is.*

Based on these words, there are no requirements of actions that need to be taken; it is simply a state of immense appreciation; it is a state of being.

Having achieved clarity on this, I gathered the courage to share my new definition, and tell some people that I was in love with them. I remember having had three conversations, each of which had a different outcome. The first one received it nicely - in fact, it was while talking to her that I got that I could create my own definitions; and it was okay if they did not coincide with the standard ones. The second person I had this conversation with, initially was very appreciative and encouraging of my full honesty, but soon distanced herself from me because, based on *her* understanding of what being in love means, she thought that I was asking her for something that she was unable to give me, even though I wasn't. The third person was an old friend of mine, who fully got where I was coming from and what I meant by those words, and who actually stated that it was reciprocal. It was a beautiful exchange of openness and appreciation for one another. The mere fact that no actions needed to be taken allowed for both of us to know that there is someone who will always love us and appreciate us deeply, even if our life paths are not to be shared any more than by contacting or meeting each other once a year, or once every few years.

My mind wonders what yours thinks as it reads these ideas, but not from a place of concern, rather from a place of curiosity. Have you ever questioned what being in love means to you? Do you believe you are capable of being in love with more than one person at a time? Can you even imagine how much broader your experience of profound love could be if you considered this as a reality? I am aware that many of my ideas are quite radical, but I believe that just by inquiring about them, you can start discovering fascinating things about yourself and your own understanding of the world.

COMING OUT TO OUR FAMILY AND LOVED ONES ABOUT OUR SEXUAL ORIENTATION AND RELATIONSHIP-STYLE PREFERENCE

I can't remember how much I shared with my loved ones during my exploration period, although I wouldn't be surprised if it was a great deal, because, as I have stated before, I used to think that not doing so created distance between us. And so, as uncomfortable as many of those conversations often were, I forced myself to have them because I also mistakenly used to feel I owed it to them.

What I do recall is how things went down from the moment I kissed the girl and my husband said he wanted to get a divorce. I was 100% open with people about what had happened; never did I try to hide my actions, nor did I avoid responsibility for what I had done, as prone to judgment as that made me.

My mom was particularly thrown off because only a few weeks before this happened we had been talking about me starting to try to get pregnant soon, so it was a very radical shift to go from talking about pregnancies to hearing that we are going to get divorced because I had discovered that I am bisexual and that exploring that side of my sexuality is not a journey that my husband was willing to be a part of.

I remembered having heard of an organization called Guimel, which was the support and empowerment group for the LGBT community within the Jewish Community in Mexico, and I thought they could be a good resource. To my pleasant surprise, it turned out that the person in charge of the parent support group was a family friend of ours from when we were younger, which immediately gave me a sense of peace and confidence in reaching out. She became an extremely pivotal and empowering source of support for me during this period.

While I was still in Florida, she and her husband met up with my family in Mexico and started exploring how they could help. First, they shared their own story -they have a son who is gay-, then, they gave them information and resources to understand what bisexuality is, and I am not sure exactly what the words she said to my mom were, but I do know that their initial interaction immediately created a sense of compassion and understanding from my mom towards me. She was able to understand that this was not me being rebellious but rather me discovering something about myself that I did not know was there.

My dad had a little harder time with it all and continued to question why I would call myself 'bisexual' if I hadn't yet been in a relationship with a woman. He thought that perhaps it was just a curiosity that would soon disappear, but to me, it was evident from the beginning that this is not the case. Up until now, I think he still hopes that this is just a phase and that I will end up with a man, in a so-called 'normal relationship'.

It has taken many conversations for them to try to understand my orientation and preferences. And, to be honest, I can sympathize with how challenging this can be for them, as I have stepped out of all the norms they are familiar with and that we grew up surrounded by, not only in the realm of sexuality but in the way my life has unfolded overall.

In addition, I know from first-hand experience, that anything that is new, unprecedented, or foreign to us can initially be scary because we have no idea what to expect. What I can -and will take this opportunity to openly- do is acknowledge both of them for being extraordinary parents who, no matter how shocked they were/are or how little they like my life choices, they have ALWAYS stayed by my side. They have made being close to me much more important than being right about the way in which I should be living my life, and I could not be more grateful for that.

I consider their response an incredible blessing because coming to terms with this new reality and with the implications this was having on my personal life was challenging enough in itself. Therefore, having to deal with parental rejection or punishment, for this reason, would have made it that much harder. They are both remarkable examples of unconditional love.

There was one thing that my mom used to say to me, that she seemed to have gotten before I did, which was: "this is not something you are *choosing* to be, but rather something you already are but you are now *discovering*, so, be kind to yourself". It took me hearing that quite a few times to actually internalize it and be okay with it, but I am grateful that there is where she stood.

I shared with my friends as well, and even though I *did* share openly, there was always the fear in the background of being judged or misunderstood. Luckily, that I can recall, that was never the case. It's funny to me, for example, that it was a big deal for me to say that I had kissed a woman, when culturally in the States it is rather common for girls to do so, whether it is out of exploration or perhaps just for fun when they're partying or whatnot. I say that it is funny because it makes me realize the huge difference our social environment can have on how we experience things. Had I grown up in a different environment, one in which embracing and expressing every aspect of our sexuality was socially acceptable -or at least, not frowned upon- perhaps the way this aspect of my life unfolded would have been different. But these types of speculations don't really take us anywhere, because the bottom line is that everything happened the way it did.

A few months after I "came out" to myself and my family -which as I shared before, happened almost at the same time- I was having a conversation with my then-roommate about what the world would be like if people could feel safe to openly talk about the things that we feel most shame about. In her case, this was to talk about her weight -because she was overweight-, and in mine, it was about me being bisexual and polyamorous. We decided to become "catalysts" for such safe space, and so we wrote a very bold post on Facebook sharing these facts with people, inviting others to share things about themselves that they felt uncomfortable talking about, with the intention and belief that all of our vulnerability would bring about freedom to ourselves, and respect and perhaps even admiration from others, more than judgment.

It was not easy for me to do that, having been conditioned by such a critical social environment growing up. But we did it. That was probably around April or May 2016. In September of that year I started traveling and ended up moving to Vietnam, and I did not go back to Mexico until July 2017. When I told my family that I was coming, one of my cousins insistently told me that he wanted to meet up and go for coffee with me. It was a little odd to me, because even though we were extremely close, he had never been so persistent to make sure we met up before I left the country again. It turned out that the reason for this was that he was going through his own process of discovery at the time, but almost nobody knew, and someone else in the family who had read my post had brought it up in a family gathering, so he knew that I was someone he could open up to about this subject.

The moment he said this to me, I thought: "just because of this single event, it was already 100% worth it to have exposed myself the way I did". I was over the moon and infinitely grateful that he felt comfortable enough to talk to me about it. And as you can imagine, having this in common brought us even closer together.

A year and a half later, I went back to visit my family again, but this time I went with my partner-at-the-time who is transgender. At this point, only my cousin's immediate family knew that he was bisexual as well, but his

103

grandparents, aunts, uncles, and cousins did not know yet. His grandparents knew that I am bisexual from the post, but we had never spoken about it with each other, nor did they know yet that my partner was transgender. So, I was having a conversation with them and at some point, they said something like "you know we know everything about you, and you know we think you are crazy, but we love you nonetheless". I saw that statement as a perfect opportunity to open up about my partner, not so much for my self-interest but rather with the intention to start creating an accepting environment for diversity for whenever my cousin decided to come out.

I said to them "there is one thing you don't know about me, and it is that my partner is transgender: he is biologically female but identifies as a man". They were startled by this information, particularly because you couldn't obviously tell just by looking at him that this was the case. They were dropping me off at home when this happened, so they just gave me a hug and left. My heart was pounding, and all my inner fears started to creep up: the fear of being looked down upon, of being rejected, of losing my dignity, of them potentially stopping loving me because of it... These same fears had shown up with other people too, but for some reason, they felt stronger this time around.

Soon after I got home, I sent them a message about how difficult it had been for me to say this to them, and all my fears, but how I did it anyway because it was important it was for me to be transparent and not feel like I needed to hide things about my life out of not wanting to be judged. Their response was amazing! They told me how all they care about is that I am happy, and however I choose to be happy does not make any difference to them. They told me that they love me for me, without conditions, and that I had nothing to worry about.

I was very moved by that response and also very hopeful about my cousin being accepted with as much love and generosity as I had been, whenever he chose to come out.

As time has passed by, and I have done more inner work, I have grown in many different ways. Talking about my sexual orientation and relationship-style preference has become easier and easier. I won't introduce myself to people saying: "Hi! I am Yael, I am bisexual and poly". But if it comes up in conversation or I see that opening up about it could make a difference to the person I am speaking to, I will talk openly about it. I still hesitate a bit before speaking about poly in particular, but I believe at this point that it is more out of habit than anything else, and I also believe that the more I continue to share about it, the more that hesitation will dissipate.

If I can leave you with one thing, it would be this:

If you have someone in your life who may be facing a similar circumstance -of having a different sexual orientation, identity, or relationship-style preference- please know that it makes all the difference in the world to them to know that your love for them is not dependent upon any of the conditions above and that you value and honor their vulnerability and courage to be true to themselves. We all have expectations and ideals of what our families could look like; it is a natural part of being human. But know that embracing the discrepancies between our expectations and reality can result in a wonderful opportunity to discover new things -about ourselves, about others and about life-, and to create the next greater version of ourselves.

If we had the freedom to choose WHO/HOW we want to be (which we do), do we want to be critical, angry, separate, and right? Or do we want to be loving, supportive, kind, compassionate, and accepting? It really is up to us. And the latter would make for much better relationships and for a much better world.

QUESTIONING AND REDEFINING LIFE

The more I have involved myself in the world of self-development, the more it has become a common practice for me to question words we use to address matters that are particularly influential on how we perceive different aspects of our lives. In addition to having redefined what it is to be in love with someone, I have challenged a few other ones such as what it means to be present in someone else's life, what being in a "stable" relationship means, etc. Doing this has come very handy because I live about thirty hours away by plane from my family and many of the people closest to me, and the common definition for being present is one that would always have me feeling far away.

In my experience, presence does not need to be physical or acknowledged in order to exist. This exploration had probably started quite a few years back since I haven't lived in the same place as my family since I was eighteen. However, it became clearer in 2018, when one of my best friends -one that I refer to as my unbiological sister- was diagnosed with terminal cancer. She had survived breast cancer a few years prior, but her cancer came back, and despite all her faith and exposure to conventional and alternative healing methods, she ended up passing away.

It was very hard for me to know everything that she was going through and accept that I was unable to be physically there with her. We did not know how long she would live –maybe it would be a few months, maybe it would be a few years–, and I was not in a financial position where I could afford to fly to be with her and to also miss work for however long it would have been. So, I started asking myself how I could be present, without physically being there.

I started sending her texts regularly, just to check in and tell her how much I loved her. Very often she would read those messages and not respond, but it was perfectly fine because at least she had seen them. When she was admitted to the hospital, I made sure to ask as many of our mutual friends that were going to visit her to give her my love, which I know they did.

A few weeks before she passed, when I heard that her condition was deteriorating more and that, at this point, it was almost inevitable that she would not survive, I reached out to a Facebook group of Mexican Women around the world. I shared with them her story and I also requested them to send their prayers, love, and energy so that my friend would have a smooth and easy transition from this life. I was completely blown away by their responses: almost 1,500 people who don't know me or her responded sending their love and blessings!

I also remember sending her texts acknowledging her, and telling her how much I admired her, and how much of an impact she had had on my life and on so many other people's lives. I would share with her my thoughts and all that I was doing with the intention to stay close to her. In addition, every night before I went to bed, I would clasp my hands together, imagining that the other hand I was holding was hers. And I still do that today. While she never verbally acknowledged any of these actions, I have no doubt in my mind or heart that she felt every single one of them. She felt the love and energy that was being sent to her every single day; she knew I was with her all along, just like she is with me.

How is she with me? I'll tell you how: so much of Who I Am today has been significantly impacted by the conversations we had over the years, and by who she was for me. There was a period during which I was trying to step into my leadership but was still dealing with many insecurities and issues, and she offered to speak to me at least three mornings a week to empower me. She did that month after month. She always interpreted me as being greater than I knew myself to be, she knew me so well. In addition, who she was and the way she lived her life set a huge example for me -and for many others- about what's possible. Ultimately, she is with me because the quality of my life has been directly impacted by having crossed paths with her.

This last statement can be expanded to everyone we have shared even small parts of our life with. Any interaction that has had even the smallest direct or indirect impact on the quality of our lives, according to my perception of the world, is present in our lives. For instance, the academic advisor that introduced me to the field of Occupational Therapy back in 2007 is currently not an active part of my life, so we could say that she is not present. However, the mere fact that she suggested I get involved in such a fulfilling profession, one that has provided me with such tremendous tools for life, makes her eternally present in my life. And I could give you many other examples. But I want to share the most relevant one for me right now: my beautiful nephew.

At the time of this writing, he is almost eight months old. I saw him when he was born, and I have not seen him (in person) since. It used to be hard for me to not think of me as a 'bad aunt' for choosing to continue living my life as I have, rather than moving back to Mexico to be near him. I considered this for a while but then tried to imagine how much time I would really spend with him every week and how I would feel the rest of the time. I knew I would be robbing myself of the freedom, financial stability, flexibility of schedule, and passion for what I do every day in the life I have created in Vietnam and concluded that the cost of being physically close to him would be too high.

Yet, I still want to be present in his life even if I am not physically there. So, I make sure to communicate with my sister-in-law almost every day to see how they're doing and let them know how much I love them. We video-call often, or they send me videos in which his mom sings a little song they made up about me so that I won't be a complete stranger. I have him as my lock-screen on my phone, and every time I see it I "say hi" to him. I am not sure how all of this is going to translate over time, but I can only hope that he will always know I love him.

As portrayed by these two examples, the fact that presence does not need to be physical or acknowledged in order to exist has allowed me to be at peace with the choices I have made. I feel at ease living my life in the way I consider best for me, knowing that I am still eternally present -even if not physically- in the lives of those I love.

Another concept I started questioning was that of being in a *stable* relationship. I was sharing with a friend about my life as it is, and the topic of love came up. I initially said that I have not been in a stable relationship since I broke up with my last partner, but immediately stopped myself and questioned: "is living with, spending lots of time with, or creating a future with someone a defining factor, such that its absence would determine that I am not in one?" In our society, I would dare to say that it is frequent for people to equal having a boyfriend/girlfriend or husband/wife with being in a stable relationship. But is it necessarily so?

I was in a relationship for almost two years. It had great moments of joy, laughter, love and appreciation, growth, fun, connection, and passion. But it also had just as many that entailed upset, anger, arguing, power-struggle, jealousy, blaming, and so forth. There was a very intense and constant shift between one and the other. Would that relationship be considered stable simply because we lived together and were planning a future?

In the next period of my life, I enjoyed a relationship with a few different people in various parts of the world, with which I was in touch regularly -even just on a bi-weekly, monthly, or yearly basis, and not daily. With them, communication is open, loving, and respectful and there is a beautiful, intimate, peaceful, and pleasant interaction every time we connect. Therefore, based on my reframed understanding of stable romantic relationships, I, indeed, am in more than one.

If I looked into other words that I could use to describe the kind of relationship I was *not* in during that period, I am certain that I would find ways to challenge those too. What I am ultimately trying to convey here is that no concept in life is fixed or unshakeable and that our experience of what it is to be alive can be positively altered when we dare to question our acquired understanding of the world around us.

As you might have gathered, this train of thought can lead to a never-ending life-inquiry that not everyone may be interested in pursuing. However, I am a strong advocate of the importance of *knowing* that we do have options. It is not the same for someone to live an unquestioned life because they have chosen not to put forth the time and effort it would take to do so than to live that way because they believe that's 'the only way possible'. Whichever way you choose, your actions may end up being the same as they would have, had you not known you had options. Yet, *where* you are taking them from will be a much more empowered place.

LEARNING LIFE LESSONS

I am a firm believer that we are not here on Earth just to take a stroll and sensorially experience what's on it; we are here to profoundly connect and familiarize ourselves with everything that *is* and that *happens* around us and within us. We are here to learn, to grow, and to make the best use of our time as we re-create ourselves into the greatest version of who we are -whatever that looks like for each of us.

During our time here, endless situations will present themselves as opportunities for us to learn lessons that will support us in achieving what we are out to accomplish. In this sense, I believe there are three main tendencies available to us, in terms of what we do with these opportunities:

1) We recognize the lessons and embrace them, internalize them, and use them as new and exciting tools that support us moving forward.
2) We recognize and embrace them, and we *think* we have learned from them, but then we find ourselves in similar situations again that have us question whether we actually did.
3) We recognize them but fight them and resist learning what they have to teach us, and thus we keep encountering them over and over again.

As someone who loves growing and developing herself, and who always aims to become the best version of herself, one of the questions I like to ask myself is;

"What can I learn from this?"

Because of this, and because of my love for journaling, I have become very self-reflective and self-aware over the years. That's why I consider I'm pretty effective at identifying the lesson in any given situation, whether pleasant or unpleasant. The challenge has been when I find myself caught in either the second or third tendencies, which I am sure many of you can relate to. Thus, I will delve into these last two.

QUESTIONING WHETHER WE HAD REALLY LEARNED THE LESSONS WE THOUGHT WE HAD

Up until August of 2019, I was in a committed relationship for almost two years. It was one of the most challenging relationships I have ever been in, on many different levels. To begin with, we started off being long-distance. We had only seen each other in person twice while I was visiting in Florida but already living in Vietnam. A few months after we met, we started chatting, then the chats turned into phone calls, and the phone calls turned into eight-hour-long video calls. While we had started talking with the intention of just getting to know each other, soon we found ourselves becoming a very important part of each other's life. We agreed to be in a committed and open relationship, especially since the conversation about polyamory was one of the aspects that had brought us together in the first place.

Things were very rocky from the beginning, and in a very short period of time, we had faced several difficulties. Many of these had stemmed from the precise topic of polyamory because he was interested in it and it was the kind of relationship he wanted, but he had never actually experienced it and was not emotionally ready for it.

This was making my time in Vietnam rather difficult. While I was still living life the way I wanted to, I simultaneously had to deal with the emotional consequences of arguing with my partner about it almost every day. Until one day I had a conversation with a friend who said: "you did not move to the other side of the world to live your life the way you want to, just to have someone in the US controlling and limiting you". As obvious as that was, I had been oblivious to it, so this was a great eye-opener that gave me the courage to start setting some boundaries.

Let me add here that this was the very first time in my life that it was me who ended a relationship. Never before had I dared to, out of fear of 'making the wrong decision' or 'not finding someone else that would be willing to put up with all my baggage'.

Before we broke up, we had planned for him to come and visit me in Vietnam, and he had already purchased his ticket. As the dates for the trip came nearer, I had no idea whether he was going to come or not. So, I decided to ask a mutual friend to find out. She told me that he was on his way. I did not hear from him until the second-to-last day he was there. He reached out, I invited him over, we had plenty of conversations about the things that had happened in the past, and were able to thoroughly enjoy each other's company for those less-than-twenty-four hours.

It was very difficult for him to leave the next day; because everything we had learned about each other that had made us want to be together in the first place had been present. He wanted to miss his flight and stay with me, but he ended up flying back to Florida and as soon as he landed, he sent me a message saying: "I am coming back. I don't want to live my life without giving this relationship a proper chance".

That was in April 2018, and I was planning on going on a six-to-eight-month trip in August of that year. So, we started looking into how the dates would work for him to come to spend time with me without it coinciding with the time when I was supposed to leave on my trip. I did not want to have to divide my attention between spending time with him and being able to have some quality time with all the people I wasn't going to see for the next while. To make the story short, he used the months before his trip to sell many of his belongings in order to be able to join me on my trip and then move to Vietnam to live with me.

Based on my previous life experiences, I clearly explained to him that I did not want him to move here *only* because of me, because I did not want to carry the responsibility of knowing that he had left everything behind just to be with me. I could not stand to feel "guilty" if at some point I wanted the relationship to end because things were not working out.

Furthermore, at that moment in his life, he did not have a steady income nor a clear career path. He had decided he no longer wanted to work just to make money. He wanted to keep searching until he found something that was meaningful and gave him a sense of purpose, while also providing for him financially. Understanding that we each have our own process and timing to figure things out, I told him he could take his time figuring out ways to generate money, AS LONG AS it did not have a financial impact on me.

Technically, he agreed to all of those conditions. We went on a six-month trip to India, Nepal, Florida, Mexico, and Israel and grew tremendously as individuals and as a couple. Even though we did have many differences during our trip, we were slowly making progress towards learning how to be together. Despite the challenges of the relationship, we had both chosen to stay, not so much *for* the other person, but for *ourselves* to be able to work through -and heal- all of these things that were coming up for us, so that we would never have to experience them again, neither with each other nor with anyone else. And ideally, the other person would get to reap the benefits of our healing. As strange as this thought was, I found it motivating, because many of the reasons why we were having issues had shown up in my previous relationships as well.

He had requested that I not see other people during the four months we were in India so that we could work on building a solid foundation for our relationship before we started to open up to other people, and I agreed to his request. However, he knew from the beginning that there was someone in Israel that I would want to see while we were there, which would be after that four-month period. As you can imagine, this did not go over very well.

Fast forward to the end of our trip. We went back to Vietnam and started our life together there. The following seven months were some of the hardest months I've experienced in my life. We kept having fights, followed by three-to-four hour-long conversations, day after day for the first four months. I expressed levels of anger that I didn't know existed in me until I eventually broke down and slipped into the worst emotional imbalance I have ever experienced.

I went to see a psychiatrist, who started me on medication again. We wanted to work with a couples' therapist, but the doctor recommended that I should not participate in any conversation that could be a trigger for almost two months. First, I needed to recover some emotional balance, so we honored his recommendation. It took me a little over two months to get back to my familiar, joyful, sociable, active, peaceful self.

Once that period ended, I started taking an active part in therapy. We were lucky to have found an extraordinary counselor, who excelled at understanding each one of us individually. I felt like I was able to understand my partner's world better, but I did not feel he was getting into mine any more than before. I was very frustrated. And so was he. He also felt like he was getting into mine, but I wasn't comprehending his.

We continued to struggle until one day everything clicked for me. I got to the source of my resentment and understood the lack of workability in the relationship. It turned out that, as much as I thought I had done the work to identify what I was looking for in a relationship, and even though I thought I had been upfront with my partner about what that was, I found myself entering and staying in a relationship that stepped on the things I considered to be crucial to making a relationship succeed.

It would be easier for me to blame him for everything: for not being financially stable and having borrowed money from me; for not feeling secure enough to be confident in being a part of a polyamorous relationship and having given me a hard time when I wanted to see someone else; for pushing for conversations that I did not want to have; for not having fully overcome his past trauma and taking things out on me as a result. For repeatedly complaining about how difficult his transition to living there had been and how lonely he felt; for having made me doubt myself and question whether I was being selfish by insisting on things being the way I wanted them to be...

However, if I blamed him, I would have no power; and my well-being would depend on him changing all of these areas that don't work for me. Instead, I accepted being 100% responsible for being in the situation that I was in; and for *not having had the courage* to stand firmly for what works for me.

The reason why the title of this section is 'Questioning whether we had really learned the lessons we thought we had' is because the end of my second marriage seemed to have been caused by me not having been fully upfront on who I was and what I wanted from the beginning. However, I was convinced that this time I had been, and yet I found myself having been better at communicating it, but not courageous enough to stand for it.

Life has a funny way of making sure that we learn what we are supposed to, by putting us in similar situations over and over again until we finally get it. I would like to say that "this time I *really* got it, and I won't repeat the same patterns again". But, as I have shared before, I have come to realize that it works better for me to hold on to beliefs that empower me, as opposed to selecting those that 'sound good'.

This is what I mean:

When I make the statement "I got this, I will never find myself in this situation again," I am creating a level of expectation that's too high, and may result in greater disappointment if I end up being there again. In contrast, I can say "I will do everything that is in my power and *in my current level of awareness* to prevent it from happening again, and, there is a chance that it will, in which case I will learn what there is to learn and come out stronger and closer to the next grandest version of Who I Am".

There is a famous quote by Maya Angelou that says:

"Do the best you can until you know better. Then, when you know better, do better"

After I got divorced both times, I discovered certain elements that had been "missing" in my assertiveness when choosing to be in a committed relationship, in order for that relationship to work. I made sure -to the best of my abilities- to put those in before I entered my next relationship. However, having discovered "certain elements" is not the same as having seen *all* the elements that were missing, and one of those that I hadn't learned from the second to the third relationship was that of setting healthy boundaries.

There is a difference between being in a *similar* situation, and being in *the same one,* which I often fail to acknowledge -and I imagine that many of you do too. In our human tendency to be extremely self-critical, we focus on the emotions that we are experiencing again, without paying close attention to the *conditions* that are leading to these emotions.

In this case, I experienced disappointment when I noticed that I found myself again being in a relationship with someone who was not ready for polyamory. But I failed to acknowledge that in my second marriage my husband had been a NO from the beginning, and, in this last relationship, my partner was a YES but turned out not to be ready for it. I was also disappointed at finding myself being with someone who was not financially stable yet. But I failed to acknowledge that when that happened with my first husband, I mostly depended on him financially, and so my whole stability depended on him. In contrast, in my last relationship, I was fully financially independent, so agreeing to be with him while he figured it out -had I not stepped over my own boundaries or acted out of guilt- would not have affected my stability.

I experienced self-doubt, which I had encountered in all my previous relationships, again. However, the extent to which I allowed my self-doubt to control my actions was different. In the past, I would have given in to accepting whatever I was told that was going on with me as my truth. But this last time, my self-doubt did not stem from accepting someone else's assertion about me as my truth, but rather from questioning the morality of what I had defined as my truth. For example, in the past, if I was told "you're acting out of fear" I would say "Oh! Maybe they're right". This time, I would not say "maybe they are right" I would say "I KNOW it is not fear but rather knowing what is important to me and what I am willing to put up with and what I am not, but I am not sure if I am a bad person for standing for it so strongly, perhaps a 'good' partner would give me more leeway".

The whole point with these examples is that I used to feel bad for experiencing disappointment and self-doubt again after all the work that I had put in, without acknowledging that the reason why those emotions were showing up had dramatically shifted. Hence, if I look at it from an objective standpoint, and from an understanding that there is always "the next level" of growth, I can see that every time I have experienced -and learned from- any of these circumstances, I have created the next grandest version of the greatest vision I have held about Who I AM.

It is almost like an endlessly-layered onion that we are gradually peeling off. Every time we peel away a layer, we get closer to the greatest version we hold of ourselves. But it is endless because the greatest version we hold of ourselves is ever-changing, just as we are.

What I invite you to do, the next time you find yourself spending your energy on feeling bad for "being in the same situation all over again" is this: Make a small shift and, instead, focus on identifying and acknowledging how the *conditions* under which this situation is happening are almost inevitably not the same that you experienced before. Most likely, if the exact same conditions were present, it would not affect you the same way it did the first time around. Therefore, be kind and bring compassion to yourself. As I mentioned before, an empowered life is about *progress*, not perfection.

FIGHTING AND RESISTING THE LESSONS

I can be a dreamer sometimes, and one of the dreams I keep holding onto, one that has been a source of different degrees of frustration for me -because I resist accepting that it is simply not possible-, is that of being able to have *everything* and be *everywhere* I want, and, being able to have/do it *all at the same time*. And I don't mean it in terms of material stuff (which large amounts of money could provide if I won the lottery). I mean it more in the sense of life paths and experiences, which have made me feel torn multiple times.

I am very aware that every decision we make in life has benefits and costs. I also realize that the decisions we make, ideally, are based on knowing -or believing- that the benefits will outweigh the costs. Furthermore, I have been reminded repeatedly that it is possible to pay the costs of our decisions with dignity, but that does not mean there will not be some sort of emotional pain involved, even if only temporarily. So I would say that all things considered, I have become pretty good at owning the costs of my decisions and not complaining about them from a victim perspective.

The challenge has been that, even if I do not complain about them -or not much outwardly-, I still struggle internally coming to terms with the fact that I can't have it all. For instance, I knew, the moment that I chose to further explore my sexual orientation, that my cost was going to be my second marriage. Was I thrilled about it? Of course not, but I was going to pay it because I knew that my personal cost in staying would have been way greater in the long run. And yet, for a while, I struggled to accept that I could not have that wonderful man by my side and still explore my individual self further. Why could not I? My love and commitment towards him hadn't changed, my desire to build a life and create a family together with him hadn't either, so why could not I have both?

I could not because that was not what he wanted. I realized that I could have him as a husband *and/or* I could have my freedom, but I couldn't have them both at the same time.

I eventually came to terms with this. I started my new life in Vietnam, focusing a large part of my energy on continuing my journey of self-discovery. I was thrilled about my choice because it had not only met but even surpassed my expectations of what exploring further would be and feel like. By choosing to live there, there was a new cost I had to pay, which was that of being thirty-plus hours away from my family. This cost I was pretty much okay with, because, as much as I adore my family, the benefits were extraordinary.

This peace only lasted for so long, however, because the inner battle started again when my nephew was born. I went into that space of "why can't I have the life I love, in this place where I am completely fulfilled, and be near my nephew at the same time?". That answer was pretty straightforward as well: I could not because the physical location where those two elements were happening was not the same. I could indeed have both, just not at the same time. In an effort to come to terms with this, I started to come up with alternative ways to be close to him, which seemed to make the distance more manageable.

In a way, I have come to realize that even if I resist whatever reality is presenting itself for some time, I eventually do accept it. So perhaps the question would be "how can I cut down the time or inner conflict that I experience until I can accept that I can't have it all?"

The problem with asking this question is that it immediately creates a self-expectation of having to come up with an answer. I was hoping that, by the time I reached this point in the narrative, I would have the perfect recipe for you to follow step-by-step, so you would not have to deal with any inner pulling, and you could move to acceptance straightaway. And what I have discovered instead is that this is a beautiful example of a situation when admitting that there are things over which we have no control comes in handy, because being ready -emotionally or spiritually ready - is one of them.

There is a quote by Joyce Meyer that says:

"The right timing is not always our timing"

I don't usually like to use the terms right or wrong, but I am using this mostly for the second part of the quote, which to me states that just because I think I should learn/know something right now, does it mean that I am ready for it or that I will. Life has shown me over and over again -in this and many other areas-, that it is not a matter of how *badly* I want something but how *ready* I am for it. And readiness does not always come at will. For instance, a baby may want to be able to walk; but if their body is not strong and coordinated enough yet, it just won't happen.

Life's timing is always perfect.

I mentioned before that I have eventually come to terms with the fact that I can not have it all -or not all at once- in regard to specific situations. I have also shared that I tend to hold on to beliefs that empower *me*, even if these are argued against by other experts. In this case, a belief that works for me is this one: the access to peace of mind lies in accepting that I don't have control over *when* the learning happens, and in learning to embrace the rollercoaster ride of emotions while it does. In the end, these ups and downs are nothing but a sign or a reminder that we are alive. Furthermore, we would not really know how to appreciate the ups as much, if we never had downs, would we?

The most recent situation I have bumped up against is that of having left Vietnam to visit my family in Mexico. I was not able to work since the beginning of February 2020 due to the Coronavirus pandemic. The virus had not reached the West yet, so my original plan was to visit friends and family for five weeks leaving at the end of February and then return to work. What I did not anticipate when I came up with that plan was that a few unexpected events were going to happen: 1) That I would meet a person with whom I want to create a life and a future. 2) That I would not be able to go back to Vietnam on the original date, even if I wanted to, because of the Covid-19 imposed travel restrictions worldwide.

Initially, the question was "why can't I be with her And continue having the life I love, with the financial stability I had attained, doing something I am passionate about and being surrounded by all the wonderful people I have met in Vietnam?". An easy answer would be "yes, you can, she can move over there with you". But when all conditions are considered, the costs of her moving to Vietnam are probably just as high as mine moving back to Mexico. And yet, assuming that we could find a way to make it work for her to be there with me, we can't get there anyway.

The bottom line is that life is telling me again: "you can have *that* life you love, and you can physically be with this extraordinary person, but you cannot do both at the same time".

There is a quote by the Dalai Lama that says:

"Remember that sometimes not getting what you want is a wonderful stroke of luck."

Let's say that it would be nice to have it all and have it all at the same time. But if I did, how would I grow? If everything I ever wanted was to be given to me on demand, I would never get to learn and practice patience, resilience, priority setting, detachment, the inevitability of impermanence, gratitude, acceptance, compassion for myself and others, etc. And if my purpose in life is to become the next grandest version of the greatest vision ever I held about who I am, I can understand and accept that each one of the elements mentioned above is a valuable contributor to that 'greatest vision'.

In this specific situation, not being able to have it all at the same time is allowing me to:

127

a) Practice letting go of my need to be in control since the borders being closed is not something I can do anything about.

b) Practice being flexible and flowing with life, understanding that circumstances may change, and thus my life-plans may too.

c) Practice healthy communication with my partner, during which we get to identify and lovingly discuss our situation, and we get to creatively come up with alternatives that work for both of us.

d) Understand how committed I am to her and to this relationship, to a degree that I am now willing to make moves that I never thought I would.

e) Open myself up to the possibility of having an extraordinarily fulfilling life elsewhere, and giving up the attachment to it necessarily having to be in Vietnam.

f) Practice embracing uncertainty and learning to be at peace with not knowing.

g) Identify grace and abundance all around me, in ways I never conceived before.

h) Practice patience and trust, and learn new ways to soothe me when anxiety or concern come up.

i) Value everything I have and had even more.

j) Practice looking for -or creating- opportunities, rather than making mountains out of molehills and drowning in fear

And the list can go on.

While I may be temporarily resisting and fighting the reality of my current circumstances, I am clearly still also growing and putting into practice wonderful life-skills. And the more I practice them, the better I become at them. I know that this "resistance" is only temporary, and I can focus my attention on embracing the emotions and the opportunities that show up in the meantime.

My fear of vulnerability would love to say that "I am masterful at radically accepting reality" in an attempt to portray a picture of absolute self-composure. However, I find it more valuable to say:

I know that there will be things that I won't like -and that you won't either-, and I know that it will take us some time to genuinely accept them. Whenever we find ourselves in one of those instances, we get to remind ourselves that:

We are always exactly where we are supposed to be, and everything is consistently and undoubtedly unfolding exactly as it should.

If that is the case, we get to take some time to acknowledge our progress within the opportunities that we are being presented with, and we get to practice gratitude and appreciation.

Our suffering comes from being attached to wanting to have control and wanting things to unfold in a particular way. And any time this is not the case -which is more often than not- we feel disappointed, frustrated, perhaps even angry. What is interesting to notice about those situations, is that experiencing any of those negative emotions *does*

129

not change the reality of those things (that is, the fact that we can't control them and that they will happen as they will).

This attachment is nothing more than a quality of being human. Thus, unfortunately -or fortunately, depending on the light we want to shine on it- it is not something that we will be able to simply make disappear one day. Unfortunately, because of course, the idea of not having attachments sounds appealing and appeasing; but fortunately, because, once again, that of not having everything resolved and easy allows us to continue to grow.

There is a quote by Buddha that says:

"You can only lose what you cling to".

I believe that the more we practice embracing uncertainty, giving up control, and acknowledging where we are and the way our life is unfolding as perfect at any given moment, the less of a sense of loss we will have over time. But remember, it is all about *progress,* not *perfection*.

THE JOURNEY OF DISCOVERING AND PURSUING OUR PASSION

The older I get, the more I think that some of the expectations that are set for us as teenagers or young adults are somewhat unreasonable in many areas of life. In this chapter, I will cover those in terms of knowing what we want to do for a living.

There are a few very fortunate people out there who, from a very young age, know what they want to do when they grow up: some doctors, actors, lawyers, architects, etc., who pursue those careers and find themselves being absolutely fulfilled from day one. But that is definitely not the case for the vast majority of us. We may have some ideas of things that we find interesting or that we think we could enjoy doing. However, the reality is that by the age we are asked to decide on a major or a career, we don't really know much about all the options that are out there -that go beyond the majors you can see listed in colleges and universities- and even less about who we are and what we truly like.

As I have mentioned before, when I was about to graduate from high school, I was certain that I was going to pursue a career in Graphic Design. I knew I liked drawing and had enjoyed some Photoshop classes I had taken. I also have a creative side that wanted to be expressed. So, when it came time to apply at a university and choose a major, that one seemed to be my best bet.

Later on, when I went to Israel and decided to move there, I started my studies at Haifa University but not in Graphic Design. Instead, -and because my choices of majors were limited by my psychometric test's score- I was doing a double major in Fine Arts and General Studies, mostly focused on Psychology. Fine Arts sounded amazing, as it involved photography, painting, drawing, and sculpting -all subjects I had always enjoyed and wanted to learn- and it seemed to go along the lines of creativity I had wanted to explore. However, it did not turn out to be a good fit for me.

I returned to Mexico and enrolled in a degree in Psychology, a subject I had thoroughly enjoyed studying while in Israel. Since I loved interacting with and helping people, I was fascinated by trying to understand the human psyche. Also, I was good at listening to others and making them feel comfortable when they opened up to me. I concluded that this would be a good fit for me. I completed the first semester and was excited about learning more, but because I became engaged to the man who was to become my first husband, and was going to be moving to Florida, I did not finish that degree either.

Once I got settled in Florida, I looked into continuing my studies, ideally in the field of Psychology. One day, I was out searching for something my brother had requested, and because I wasn't familiar with the area yet, I accidentally ended up making a wrong turn and reaching a university. I went in to ask for information and was told they did not offer a degree in Psychology and suggested I look into

Occupational Therapy. I had never heard of this field nor did I fully understand what it was, but it seemed to be a good alternative and satisfied my needs.

It turned out to be the perfect fit for me, much better than any of the others I had explored before. It actually encompassed some aspects of the other ones that I enjoyed the most, such as the outlet for creativity and the interaction with people. This made it absolutely enriching. I had truly and accidentally, discovered something I was utterly passionate about:

Supporting and empowering people to have the best quality of life possible.

I am clear that this can also be attained through Psychology. However, the means through which it is achieved are different. Being able to accomplish this through the clients' engagement and participation in meaningful and creative activities was significantly more attractive to me than doing it through conversations, and yet, I did not know this existed as an option before.

I pursued this career for about eight years and loved every minute of it. I worked in a few different clinics that practiced various approaches to treatment, and each one of them helped me grow both personally and professionally. Because of the nature of my job and how compatible it was with my passion -and putting aside some common work-related challenges that I faced throughout- I looked forward to going to work every day.

Needless to say that no job is all peachy; there were days that were harder than others, some patients that would show greater or faster progress than others. However, every little thing they accomplished was acknowledged and celebrated and made up for the not-so-fun times.

It was during this period that I started becoming aware of how many things we take for granted, which led to me making it a point to start practicing gratitude on a more conscious level. As an example, I used to work with a little eight-year-old who was born with Angelman Syndrome, a genetic disorder that affects the nervous system and had severely impaired her cognition and physical abilities. She was completely dependent on her mother for absolutely everything, except walking. During our sessions, we started working on her helping her mom take her shirt off when she needed to get changed or undressed. After weeks of practice, she was able to pull it off her head and arms if it was already partially pulled up. Her mom was extremely joyous and excited when she saw that her daughter could now participate in something as simple as that. It may not have radically altered the quality of their lives, but I am positive it definitely was a stride towards it.

As I mentioned before, each clinic had distinct approaches to treatment, thus the types of progress that we noticed were different as well. In one clinic, for example, the great accomplishment was to get a five-year-old who, due to the way he had so far developed neurobiologically-speaking, was not interested in connecting or interacting with people, to start to purposefully engage and participate in play with us (therapists) first and then with his parents as well. The progress was different, but nevertheless always extremely rewarding. No doubt about it, my years working as an Occupational Therapy Assistant were extraordinary.

By this point in the narrative, you have probably gathered that another passion of mine is traveling, so once I started traveling, I did not want to stop. And since working in the field of Occupational Therapy in Vietnam was not an option, the easiest and most feasible way for me to make a living on that side of the world was by teaching English. It was not the first time in my life that I did so, -I had taught in Mexico back in 2006 and also sporadically during the time I lived in the States- but it certainly was a great reminder of how much I enjoyed it and how passionate I was about it.

I had not particularly identified it as such at the beginning, but I later realized that teaching was yet another means through which my passion for supporting and empowering people to have the best quality of life could be manifested. Providing people with tools that will open up their opportunities in the future most definitely impacts the quality of their lives; because they were not only being taught a language but they were also being supported in developing self-confidence, empowered to ask questions if there were things they did not understand or wanted to know more of -which as obvious as this may seem, it is not commonly or comfortably practiced by students in Vietnam-. They were exposed to and had the opportunity to practice methods that unlocked their potential and allowed them to see that they are that much more capable than they may have thought; and they were given tools for *learning how to learn* that expanded beyond language acquisition, which in itself was missing for them as well.

This was another field that I thoroughly enjoyed; that I felt enlivened by, which allowed me to develop myself both personally and professionally, and that was an extraordinary channel for my creativity to come out as well. I spent three and a half years teaching in Vietnam, and I authentically visualized myself doing that long-term.

However, life seemed to have other plans for me. I shared before how, because of the Coronavirus pandemic, what was initially a five-week trip to Mexico has turned into an indefinite one, since we don't know how soon the borders will be reopened, and the magnitude of the spread of the virus in Mexico would not make it enticing for Vietnam to receive people coming from this country anytime soon anyway.

This was not an easy reality for me to come to terms with initially, to the extent that I had a depression relapse because I felt like my options of pursuing my passion while doing something that provided me with financial stability and quality of life, were being - even if temporarily- unexpectedly and inevitably shut down.

Yet, as I have mentioned before, life has taught me over and over again that, no matter how difficult things seem, everything always falls into place and I am always taken care of. It's hard for me to stay present to these facts during my neurochemical imbalances, but once they get back under control, it becomes evident again.

My family owns an insurance agency that's been up and running, supporting people, for fifty years now. It was started by my grandfather, who passed away a few years ago. Then my grandma joined in, then my uncle, my mom, my older brother, and most recently my middle brother as well. I never ever thought that I would end up being part of the business, as generous and profitable as I knew it to be; I always thought "that's not for me, that's not something I would ever work in". And I laugh now when I think of having said 'never' because throughout my life I have been reminded that *"you should never say never"* because, in almost every area that I have, I have ended up experiencing or doing many of the things that I thought or said that I wouldn't do.

The pandemic presented me with the opportunity to once again question and reframe my mindset; if I had said that my passion of supporting and empowering people to have the best quality of life possible could be also expressed through Psychology, even though I was choosing Occupational Therapy and then Teaching instead, it must mean that there may be endless other venues through which it can be expressed as well. And why would providing people with something today (such as a life insurance policy) that would guarantee that the financial needs of their loved ones will continue to be taken care of if they were to pass away couldn't be one of them?

I believe it can. And it looks completely different from anything I have ever done before, but that does not mean it can't be wonderful and tremendously rewarding as well.

Benjamin Franklin said:
"Out of adversity comes opportunity."

This global situation certainly came to turn my life around. It initially seemed frightening and at moments unfair, after all, it had taken for me to finally create a life that worked for me and was fulfilling in every way, to have to somehow start over. However, I then remembered that something good can be found in *any* situation, no matter how bad it looks, and so I chose to start shining the light on the blessings that had come out of it and the opportunities that were opening up instead. This project we are creating has a huge potential to positively impact many people's lives, but it also opens up the opportunity to closely work and create empowering partnerships with family members, which may not have been available -or even considered- had it not been for the pandemic that had me stay in Mexico longer than planned.

Over the past couple of months, I have been hearing many people say that this situation is a wonderful opportunity for people and businesses to reinvent themselves. It's quite a radical and unfortunate way to prompt that reinvention I would say, because of all the lives that are being negatively affected or that are ending because of it. But nevertheless, it can certainly be seen as a gift.

Albert Einstein said:
"Adversity introduces a man to himself."

It is during challenging times that we discover -or are reminded of- our abilities and capacities, both those that work and those that don't work for us. In this instance, however, I want to focus on the ones that work. The current situation is reminding me of (or re-introducing me to) my adaptability and resilience. I may have had a depressive relapse, but I did not stay there, and I fairly quickly started creating again. The project we're starting to work on is of a kind and potential magnitude that I did not know myself capable of managing or participating in, yet the more we advance on it and the more it demands of me, the clearer the picture becomes of how much more I am capable of than I know now. And whether this project ends up taking off as we are intending or not, the new skills, knowledge, and experiences I will acquire along the way will have certainly shaped me into a greater version of myself and will support me in any future pursuit of my passion.

There is one more quote I want to bring up here, from Srikumar Rao, which states:

"Invest in the process, not the outcome."

All we can ever do is invest our heart and soul, time, energy, effort, and resources in the process of making whatever we consider important to us -or we are passionate about- happen. Life is not so much about whether the outcome comes to fruition -or it does in the way we intend it to- since outcomes are out of our control; life is rather about who we will become and the lives we will touch in the process of making things happen.

CONFRONTING AND OWNING HOW MUCH OF OUR LIVES HAS BEEN RULED BY OUR FEARS

"Fear and Love are the same thing. <u>All fear is an expression of love</u>: love of life, love of the self, and love of others. If we did not love life, the self, or others (in other words, if we did not care about anyone or anything), we would be afraid of nothing. We would not even be concerned with our own survival."

Neale Donald Walsch

I am using this quote as an opening for this chapter to create a new context from which I will be speaking about the fears I have experienced and how they have impacted my life. To me -and hopefully to you too- this new perspective automatically brings a level of self-compassion; not because it justifies fear has ruled my life thus far, but yes because it allows me to understand where it stemmed from and realize how unclear I was on what its purpose was.

We tend to use or think of fear and love as opposite emotions, but to me, it makes perfect sense that one is an expression of the other. If Paul and Rina did not love feeling well and healthy, he would not fear being bitten by a

141

scorpion that he knows can cause him pain, nor would she fear putting on weight that she knows would make her feel unwell. If George didn't love people's approval, he would not be afraid of being out on the stage and potentially making a mistake or making a fool of himself. If Carla did not love her parents and did not care about them being proud of her, she would not fear getting bad grades or failing an exam. If Stephen did not love life, he would not be afraid to die.

Now I'm going to give you some examples that are a bit more extreme, and I remind you that this perspective is for mere understanding and <u>not</u> to condone any behavior. If someone did not love his family, he would not fear not being able to provide for them; or if he did not love having money, he would not fear not having it and would not resort to stealing. If a country's government did not love to be in control and feel powerful, it would not fear not being in control and would not turn to wars as a means to prevent that from happening. Do you get what I mean?

I know this perspective can be argued from various standpoints, and my intention is not to convince you that this one is "the truth" but rather to invite you to consider a different outlook, and inquire whether this is one that works for you. Funnily enough, sometimes the love of being right or comfortable where we are can keep us from opening up to giving thought to new points of view because we fear that our viewpoint could be 'threatened' or that our current level of comfort could disappear.

The situation, with all of the above examples and all the personal ones I will share, is that we tend to miss what the *purpose* of fear is, and hence we use it -or rather, let it use us- in unproductive ways.

The purpose of fear is not to keep us from acting or from being exposed to seemingly threatening situations, it is merely <u>to build in a bit of caution</u> as a tool that helps keep our bodies alive. Thus, fear is not to be feared; rather it is to be welcomed and looked at to see *what caution it advises.*

Considering the above to be the purpose of fear, the first question I would ask myself when I start to feel fear creeping up is: What would happen if what I fear happens? Then, I would follow it by asking: Would the next grandest version of the greatest vision ever I held about Who I Am assume that 'what could happen *will undoubtedly* happen' and let the fear control me? Or would I step into the fear and explore what there is on the other side of it?

This last question is related to what I have mentioned in previous chapters related to what my soul's purpose is. And I can truly say that, since I have become clear of what that is, it's become easier to navigate through life; to make choices, and -most importantly- to dare.

As I am writing this, I hear a part of me wishing I had gotten this awareness twenty years ago; since I believe it would have saved me a lot of trouble. But as Lao Tzu said:

"When the student is ready, the teacher will appear"

If I did not know or understand any of these concepts and ideas twenty or fifteen or ten years ago, it is merely because I was not ready for them then. And if there are things you didn't know or understand until now it is because you were not ready for them either. As challenging as it can be to accept this fact sometimes, life's timing is *always* perfect.

Prior to this new awareness, I had a different perspective on the subject of fear, which I believe turns out to complement the new one nicely. I thought that, just like everything is ever-changing, so is the *nature* and *intensity* of our fears. As we grow, we are faced with new life circumstances -or maybe with the same old ones but we, as individuals, have evolved- and are impacted by them in constructive or destructive manners. The essence of -and the power that- each specific fear exerts over us overtime may:

a) Remain at the same in intensity, but the way it controls our behavior manifests differently.
b) Decrease in intensity but continue to control our behavior.
c) Decrease in intensity but no longer control our behavior.
d) Dissipate.

Perhaps when we were very little, we were afraid of seeing or being bitten by an insect. Thus, if we saw one we would scream like crazy and run away. As we have grown older, we may:

a) Still scream but attempt to kill it instead of running away.
b) Not scream but still run away.
c) Not scream or run away, simply be wary of it and continue doing what we are doing.
d) Merely acknowledge its presence and go about our day.

This is a very simplified example of a fear, but if we are willing to look into our lives, I am positive that we can all identify more 'complex' or 'life-impacting' ones, and that we would be able to fit our response to them over time into one of the four instances described before. Let's explore this together with an example of my own life.

Ever since I first got married, at the age of 21, I was terrified about the idea of having kids. I have always thought that becoming a mom would change my life drastically; that life would no longer be about what I want or need but about what my child or children do or need. That I would lose my independence and would no longer be able to do what I want when I want to... and lazy days in bed? Forget about that! they would be over forever. I feared that I would feel restricted and thus resentful, and so during my first marriage, I didn't even feel ready to engage in conversations about it. I used to attribute this fact to how young I felt I was, but as I discovered later on, it was simply an expression of my love for my freedom, independence, and for an aversion towards greater responsibilities.

When my relationship with the one who became my second husband started to become more serious, we had conversions about becoming parents in the near future, and we planned our engagement and wedding accordingly. I was going to move forward with it, and then -as you already read in previous chapters- that marriage ended as well, because of unrelated reasons, but consequently motherhood did not happen then either.

Looking back, I am grateful it did not happen. Partly because we ended up getting divorced -and I would love for my kids to have their parents be together in a mutually respectful, loving, and fulfilling relationship-, but mainly because I realized that I had never questioned whether I wanted to be a mom or not, and I was just going to do it because "that's what you do after you get married". The option of not being a mom did not exist in my world, so unconsciously, I was feeling obligated to do something I had not even chosen; as if though I would have just been doing it simply by default.

Why hadn't I questioned it, you may ask? The main reason was fear, the same fear that, as you will see, has strongly hindered and negatively impacted many areas of my life. First, I was afraid of finding out that I did not want to be a mom. If this were the case, I was afraid that it would be the wrong choice and that I would regret it at some point, when it is already too late. Furthermore, I feared that my family's reaction would be a negative one and that my parents would be disappointed in me because they were looking forward to being grandparents. I was afraid that everyone in the community would single me out and make me feel I was wrong for deliberately choosing not to have children.

Applying the principle of fear being an expression of love in these fears, I can say that I was afraid of finding out that I did not want to be a mom because I loved feeling 'normal' and choosing not to be a mom was outside of the norm. I was afraid it would be the wrong choice and that I would regret it because I love making choices that lead to no regrets. I feared that my family's reaction would be a negative one because I love them and want to have their love, affection, and acceptance.

"We don't fear the unknown, we fear what we think we know about the unknown" - Teal Swan

What I think I know of the unknown of being a mom does not sound too attractive, and what I thought I knew of the unknown of what would happen if I were to discover that I did not want to be a mom is quite terrifying too, isn't it? What I find most fascinating, especially about the latter, is the fact that all of the fears mentioned above were nothing but *blind spots* for me; they were running my life and my actions and I had no idea they were there!

It was after the second divorce that I started to distinguish them. And the moment I did, I allowed myself the space to question whether motherhood was something I genuinely wanted.

I spent the next ten months of my life in the inquiry and exploration of whether this was something I preferred. What was interesting about this period is that, simultaneously, I was thoroughly exploring my freedom and living life "under my own terms", thus all those fears of responsibility and limitations that I mentioned at the beginning of the chapter were showing up loud and clear. Nevertheless, and after a thorough inner-search, I arrived at the conclusion that the type of bond that exists between a parent and a child was not something I wanted to miss out on.

Life works in such mysterious ways that the following relationship I had was with a transgender man. We were having conversations about becoming parents, and I used to laugh at the fact that I was now in a position in which becoming a mom would have to be a fully conscious and intentional act; that the option of getting pregnant "by mistake" (meaning that the condom would break or something) was not true for me anymore. I was amused by this fact, yet grateful because of all the inner-growth it would entail.

If we do a recap and relate it back to the four ways in which fears may exert power over us: during my first marriage, the fear of motherhood was intense and was controlling my behavior in the way of avoidance. During my second marriage, it was probably just as intense, but instead of avoiding it I was "forcing" myself to do it by having set a date by when we would already be parents. In the third instance, the fear was not as intense because I had already chosen that I wanted to be a mom, and it's hard to say whether it was controlling my behavior in any way because we had set a date for a few years down the road, so there was no pressure.

Fast forward to the present. I have been told by a physician that my ovarian reserve is low, so I have to either freeze my eggs or get pregnant as soon as possible. The fear of what I think of the unknown that is to be a mother remains, but in a much lesser intensity, and it is no longer controlling my behavior. So much so, that I have chosen to freeze my eggs now and get pregnant as soon as I finish my psychiatric treatment -which is within five months from now- , *even if* that meant that I would be a single mom. Luckily, I am in a committed relationship with an extraordinary woman, and G-d willing that will not need to be the case. Nevertheless, the essence of my fear of motherhood and the power it exerts over me has undoubtedly shifted over time.

There's a quote by Zig Ziglar that says:

F.E.A.R has two meanings:
Forget Everything And Run
Or
Face Everything And Rise
It's your choice
-   Zig Ziglar

And at this point, I am choosing the latter.

I would like to share a few other situations in which my misunderstanding of the purpose of fear controlled my behavior so that perhaps you can identify with one of them and discover a new course of action you can take.

As I shared with you in the chapter on Facing and Challenging Self-Limiting Beliefs, I did not pursue my dream of traveling back when I was nineteen or twenty out of fear of not being able to provide for myself financially on my own if I stopped receiving my parents' and the government's support. Love for *what* was this fear expression of? Love for feeling certainty, security, familiarity, for having someone to depend or rely on financially, for feeling pity for myself and seeing myself as small and incapable. It may sound odd that I would love those last few things, but the truth is that there was a huge payoff that I got out of it; I was able to stay comfortable AND did not have to be fully responsible for myself and my choices. Avoiding responsibility can be so easy and convenient! But it certainly limits people's growth, thus it is something I am no longer committed to.

I had also mentioned that I always wanted to keep a low profile, both in the way I dressed and in the way I acted, because I was afraid of people speaking poorly of me or pointing me out to judge me otherwise. Love for what was this fear expression of? Love for fitting in, feeling accepted; love for my dignity, my image, my reputation... because, at that point, my self-worth depended on people's opinion of me. I did not see or know my own worth just yet, thus, unnecessarily exposing myself to people's judgments -by being freely self-expressed in my words, actions and appearance- was an ongoing threat to my value as a person. Oh! And also, I loved control; I thought that I could control people's views of me by modifying or limiting my own behaviors. That is quite ambitious of me, isn't it?

It is easy for me to find these beliefs to be absurd now, since I have shifted so much both my perspective of myself and of life over the years, but it is almost confronting to realize how much a low self-image or self-esteem can affect a person's attitudes and experience of people and life. And yet, it simultaneously creates an awareness of what some elements that will be important to strengthen and empower my kids are, so that they won't have to face the same struggles I've had.

This last statement creates an opportunity to understand a new fear I just noticed that I am dealing with, which is the fear of not being a good mom or messing up as a mom. Love for what are these words an expression of? First of all, love for my kids -even though they have not been born yet-. Secondly, love for feeling satisfaction, fulfillment, and pride from the things I accomplish. In addition, it is love for doing things right and for avoiding making irreversible mistakes, and again, love for control.

So let's answer the questions I brought up before in regards to this fear: what would happen if what I fear becomes real? If I do not feel satisfaction, fulfillment and pride from the choices I made or the way I raised my children? My initial thought is that they would still turn out just fine, just like I did. I can almost be sure that my parents and every other parent have made choices they do not feel proud of, and yet their kids still have the possibility to turn things around for themselves and grow to live a fulfilling life, just like I have. But let's say that they *don't* turn out just fine, and that they end up being troublemakers. My next idea is that those instances that did not lead to the results I would have hoped for can be looked at as opportunities to learn and grow; and if believed to be perfect -just like everything is in life- there can even be gratitude and peace in knowing that, as unpleasant as it may seem at the moment, whatever is happening is for the best. Furthermore, I can become a victim and feel sorry for myself and for what I have 'caused' my kids, after having destroyed myself with negative self-talk, OR, I can decide to be responsible for my actions and for doing the best I could at any given moment, and I can create compassion and kindness towards myself, just like I have towards my parents.

Would the next grandest version of the greatest vision ever I held about Who I Am assume that 'what could happen *will undoubtedly* happen' and let the fear control me? or would it step into it and explore what there is on the other side of it? At this point, it would certainly step into it.

This chapter could easily be indefinitely expanded, as I have faced a ridiculous amount of fears over time and I could also borrow other people's fears to give you examples, but I trust that what I have shared so far has already provided access for you to create a new relationship with fear.

I would now like to share with you some quotes and the topics that have been empowering for me:

"Feel the fear and do it anyway!" –
Jillian Michaels

If we expect fear to fully disappear before we take action, we will probably die waiting because who we naturally are is Love, so we will always love something - and thus we will always fear something. It is not about *not* fearing; it is about understanding where that fear is coming from, what it's purpose is, and then, with that new awareness, powerfully choosing whether to take action anyway.

"Decide that you want it more than you are afraid of it "
- Bill Cosby

If we were to choose not to take action, let's have it be because we authentically realize that it is not something we want or that is in alignment with Who We Are. Otherwise, let's have our preference of being that greater version of ourselves be stronger than our fear of it, whatever that "it" is.

"Let your faith be bigger than your fear"
-   Hebrews 13:6

If everything else fails -or even if it doesn't fail but you are a person of faith in something greater than yourself that has you always be taken care of- have faith in *knowing,* simply by looking back at how everything you have feared and faced in your own life has turned out, that whatever the outcome is of you stepping into the current fear will be for the best, even if you don't understand it right away.

GETTING COMFORTABLE WITH GIVING UP CONTROL

My need for control has shown up in my life multiple times throughout the years, in many different scenarios. From not ever wanting to get drunk or use drugs because I did not want to lose control; to modifying the way I dressed and monitoring the way I moved in an aim to control others' opinions of me; from wanting for my partners to be and act -or not be nor act- in particular ways in order to have me feel comfortable and secure in my relationship with them, to getting frustrated and upset because five months had gone by and I was still unable to return to Vietnam due to the pandemic, which is a circumstance out of my control ... My nature and my instinctive way of acting and reacting tends to be one that is in a constant search for control.

Thankfully, and as I have shared in other chapters, I have been in an ongoing process of developing levels of self-awareness that allows me to distinguish ways of acting and being that work for me from those that don't, and it has become clear that being reactive and controlling is one that doesn't.

Here is a list of a few reasons why needing to be in control does not work:

1) It can lead to unnecessary experiences of frustration and upset because we realize

155

that, more often than not -and no matter how hard we try-, most of the things that happen are not in our control.

2) It can negatively impact -or even destroy- relationships because it demonstrates an inability to accept that other people are different from the way we are (we want them to act the way we want them to, or the way we would), and so it creates unfair and unproductive expectations towards them that they will never be able to live up to.

3) It can take away our inner-peace and even our sleep, because we spend so much of our time and energy trying to find ways to avoid what-we-believe-could-happen-if-we-don't-control-the-situation, from happening.

4) It can bring about unfavorable emotions in us, such as anger, aggressiveness, manipulation, spitefulness, etc., in an aim to gain the control we believe we should have. And these undoubtedly affect the people we love in adverse ways.

I can think of more reasons, and I am pretty sure you could too, but I think these are enough for now to see that it's definitely not fruitful.

By no means can I say that I do not instinctively hope for control anymore, because I would be lying. However, I can say that there has been a gradual shift in me over the past five or so years that is allowing me to cope with it better.

It started during my relationship with my second husband, who was a very spiritual person. He was very much involved in energy healing, coaching, personal growth and development, and having a strong spiritual connection with G-d or a Higher Power, however each person understood it. By that time, my relationship with G-d was almost nonexistent; I would just say "God forbid something negative happens", but it was more out of habit than out of me having any sort of relationship with a Higher Power.

I used to struggle a lot with anxiety and fear of the unknown, and as part of the emotional support that my now-ex-husband provided me with, he started encouraging me to write letters to G-d, turning my worries, concern, fears, and need for control over to Him/Her, asking to get my back. This did not mean that I would stop taking the actions that I deemed possible or appropriate, but it did mean that I would let go of my attachment to the outcome and trust that whatever would happen would be for the greater good.

I followed his advice and I started to feel some weight come off my shoulders. Because of my innate controlling personality, I didn't always manage to fully let go and trust right away. However, I can joyfully admit that it has improved over time.

The next radical leap in this regard happened a few years later when I learned a new definition of what codependency is that fits me perfectly. I had heard the word *codependency* plenty of times before, but I never really identified with being codependent until I read Melody Beattie's definition:

"A codependent person is one who has let another person's behavior affect him or her, and who is obsessed with controlling that person's behavior"

I did not realize that obsessively wanting to control someone else's behaviors, whether that obsession turned into actions or remained as thoughts, was codependency. Once I got it, the whole world opened up for me, because I was suddenly able to put a name to one of the strongest sources of suffering, I had been dealing with on a daily basis. Furthermore, a powerful tool that guided me on how to fight this suffering had become available through the book and workbook named Codependent No More: I started working the Twelve Steps.

Was I going to be working the Twelve Steps!? The ones I had always associated with people who have problems with alcohol and addictions, which I don't have!? Was I going to be saying "Hi, I am Yael and I am Codependent" at a meeting and have everyone respond to me "Hi Yael" synchronously!? I never imagined that I would ever be in that position, so it was shocking initially. But it turned out to be one of the most profoundly liberating tools I have ever come across.

Step One, admitting that I am powerless over others and that my life had become unmanageable, was the most radical and empowering step for me. Why? Because I did not have to try anymore! I no longer had to keep trying to find or think of different ways in which I could change others to be something or someone that worked for me. I used to think that I had that power; I used to think that by doing -or not doing- certain things or being -or not being- particular things, I could modify or control how others behaved or felt towards me. But guess what!? That was NEVER the case nor would it ever be! So, for the first time in my life, I was able to give myself a break and breathe.

It may sound easy or obvious for some of you, but for those of you who have codependent tendencies like I do, it is a really big deal. It is not up to us for other people to change; we are only responsible for ourselves, and for nobody else. However, there is a difference between intellectually 'knowing' this to be the case, and 'knowing' because we feel to our bones that this is the case.

I would dare to say that that was a turning point in my life. Not because my codependent traits disappeared, but because I started to distinguish when they were kicking in and was no longer blindly controlled by them. Once I started working the Twelve Steps myself, I understood that of "turning my life and struggles over to G-d" (as my ex had taught me to do) at a whole new depth. Coming to believe that a power greater than me could restore me to sanity (Step Two) and making the decision to turn my will and life over to the care of God as I understood God (Step Three) were also extremely useful. Perhaps in terms of actions, the way these two steps looked remained the same as before - I still wrote letters to G-d- but the place where I was writing them from was a much more humble one. It takes a level of humbleness to accept that we are not and *will not be* in control, and also to believe that there is someone or something greater than us that could support us.

The rest of the steps are also incredibly helpful in developing and strengthening an awareness that allows me to see where my actions come from. However, I will not elaborate on them here. What I want to leave you with regarding this topic is the following:

a) Working the Twelve Steps can benefit *anyone*, not just addicts, alcoholics, or even codependents. It is a wonderful tool to feel comfortable giving up control. I may be mistaken, but I believe that, to an extent, we all deal with a need for control and certainty. It is part of being human. And what is great about this is that it is not a religious tool but a merely spiritual one; it does not speak about a specific God, it simply refers to a power greater than ourselves, whatever we choose that to be for each one of us.

b) Often people say that believing in God -or in anything other than ourselves, for that matter- is like using a crutch, where we give some of our responsibilities away, and it is usually a statement that has a negative connotation. My take on that is that, if believing in something can yield us some inner-peace and comfort, and can actually provide us with the confidence to move forward with our actions knowing that we will be taken care of, then who cares!? As long as we don't use such beliefs as a means to justify actions or behaviors that harm other people, whatever we do -or choose to believe in- to attain some inner-peace is perfectly acceptable.

c) There is no room to feel shame for being codependent or for participating in any of the programs that work the Twelve Steps. In fact, there is no room to feel shame for dealing with Anything that we deal with! Sharing about the things that we struggle with and the methods we are trying out to get past these struggles shows nothing but a person's commitment to living their best lives, being the best version of themselves, and them putting in a continuous effort to achieve so. Rawness is beautiful, Vulnerability is admirable. I invite you to acknowledge those people who have the courage to open themselves up, and to give yourself the opportunity to do so as well.

Up until a few years ago, I still believed that if I did not hear people's stories, it meant that it was because they did not have challenges and I was one of the few unlucky - or lucky- ones who did. Unlucky because I thought they had an easier life than I did, but lucky because I evolved to see every event as an opportunity to learn, grow and become a better version of myself. What I have discovered over the years, however, is that not because they don't talk about the things they grapple with does it mean that they don't have any struggles. It simply means that some of us naturally feel a bit more comfortable sharing ourselves than others, but that with a bit of vulnerability and willingness on our part to be present in their world, they can get to feel secure and choose to open up as well. We *could* go through life with strong armors and walls to keep us protected; sharing just what's indispensable. But it is that much more enjoyable and fulfilling to travel this life-journey allowing people in and sharing it with them.

Going back to the topic of control. I have recently achieved yet another level of comfort with giving it up. I first believed it was all up to me; then I started to reach out to a Greater Power but still underneath thinking I had a say. Then, I admitted to having no control over others, and from a more humble place continued to reach out to G-d. Next was discovering a whole new definition of what having *faith* is.

I am going to preface this by saying that I learned this through some Jewish teachings on *emuná* (or faith); but I believe this definition can easily be broadened to any Greater Power that anyone believes in. I always had the idea that when people would say "have faith" they referred to *blind faith*; that which is not based on experience, which requires no analysis or questioning, just believing it will happen. But through this seminar I learned that Judaism does not ask you to believe blindly; it encourages you to look back at your life and at everything that surrounds you (nature, people around you, your own body, etc.), and through mere observation of the perfection with which everything works, we can get present to the presence of a Greater Power. You don't have to be Jewish to believe this; if you pay attention to the whole world around you, you can see how - whether we understand it at the moment or not- everything always works out and it works out for the better.

It is a matter of the lenses you look through though; we always find evidence for what we look for. If you want to use a negative lens and consider my former statement inapplicable to your life (meaning that you do not consider that everything that has happened in your life has been for the better, even if it did not seem so at the moment), you will find plenty of evidence to argue with me and prove that what I am saying is not accurate. However, if you want to use a positive lens, one with which you look for the opportunity to learn and grow from everything that has happened in your life -both pleasant and unpleasant events- you will realize that a greater power has been there all along, supporting you all the way through to this moment in your life. And the moment you can see His/Her/Its presence in your entire past and present, there will be no doubt in your mind that you will continue to experience it in your future as well.

Now I have a new relationship with the word 'faith', which in turn gives me the certainty and security - based on former experience -that things are going to turn out. Perhaps not the way I think they will or I would want for them to; perhaps it's not going to happen when I would want for it to. But it will happen at the perfect moment and in the way that's best.

There is a quote I have by my mirror that says:

"The master's level of awareness includes the certainty that all outcomes are perfect, just as they are, exactly as they arise, precisely as they present themselves to serve the agenda of every soul, in every situation, in every moment, in every place"
- Neale Donald Walsch

I used to have my walls covered with quotes that were empowering at different times in my life. This last one has come to sum up all I need to remember at any given moment to stay at peace.

Keeping all of this in mind, most recently I had another huge realization regarding control, in this case *self-control*. I got that:

I do not ever need to force myself to do <u>anything</u>.

If it is something that is in my greatest interest, it will happen, and whenever it does, it will feel completely natural.

I am going to give you three recent examples in which this became completely evident:

1) I had always been attached to having long hair. I used to think of it as like my "security blanket"; what made me feel a bit more comfortable in my skin and what made me look feminine. Through the years, the thought of cutting it short crossed my mind multiple times, but every time I thought of it, it was anxiety provoking so I would end up dismissing the idea. Last week, I had a 'vision' in which I saw myself having short hair and loving it. I shared it with my girlfriend and she immediately booked an appointment for me to get my haircut the next day, before I changed my mind. It turned out that I absolutely loved the way it looked, having it short, and most strangely, I did not miss my long hair at all! Not when taking a shower, not when styling it. It was just the next natural step for me to take.

2) My family has an insurance business that's been in the market for about fifty years. My grandfather, who passed away a few years ago, started it. My grandma, mom, uncle and two brothers all work there, and while my mom always told me how rewarding and profitable it was, It was not something I was interested in doing and I always assured that I would not work there. Fast forward, the Coronavirus happened, and I unexpectedly ended up moving back to México. My brother brought up the opportunity to develop a project together (insurance-related but that

does not necessarily require one-on-one insurance selling) and I am fascinated working with him on it. I did not want to work with my family in the past, and I did not force myself to do it, but life circumstances lead to it happening, and now it feels like the natural next thing for me to do.

3) Motherhood! I have already shared with you my journey in this subject; I told you how I was terrified of it for the longest time, how I first avoided it, then was forcing myself to do it, and then wasn't sure of whether I wanted to be a mom or not. I went through all sorts of stages in this regard.

   While I had plans with my former partner to have a baby by 2022, it was still far away enough that I would not consider like I was forcing myself to do it anymore. I had actually said to myself, prior to setting that date, that I was not going to pressure myself to become a biological mom just because 'I was getting older'; that I was going to do it whenever I felt ready for it, even if that ultimately meant adopting instead of giving birth. Thus, I was allowing my life to unfold as it would.

   Most recently, what I already mentioned happened (that of me having a low ovarian reserve for my age), and so all of a sudden, I found myself in a situation in which I did need to make a choice fast. Having to make a choice was sort of forced in a way, due to the natural progression of human biology, but I could have chosen not to do it or to freeze the eggs for the future and did not. I chose to go ahead with the process, and it genuinely feels like the next natural step for me to take in my life.

The bottom line is this: there is no need to suffer or to push ourselves to do things that we think we should be doing or could be good for us, in an attempt to control our future and outcomes. Let's give up control, have faith, and KNOW that whatever needs to happen will happen at the perfect time.

LEARNING TO TRUST OUR INTUITION AND TO LIVE IN ALIGNMENT WITH OURSELVES

"A musician must make music, an artist must paint, a poet must write, if he is to be ultimately at peace with himself"
- Abraham Maslow

This is such a simple and obvious statement, yet, more often than not, not lived by. We may know what our passion is; we may know what we thoroughly enjoy doing, but we find ourselves doing something that is not *'that'*. Abraham Maslow's quote encompasses what I consider to be the single greatest lesson I have learned about life, and the key to living at peace with myself.

There are many philosophers, writers, communicators and inspirational speakers out there, and I would dare to say that there is something valuable that we can get from every single one of them. It may be that after seeing/reading/ listening to them we get something new for ourselves that we would want to do or be; and it may also be the case that we suddenly get clear on things to do or ways of being that we certainly *don't* want for ourselves.

When the latter happens, entering those people's worlds turns into opportunities for us to start discovering or defining ways of being or acting we would like to embrace.

There is one particular speaker that stands out for me, Abraham Hicks, from whom I learned what I consider to be the main access to living a fulfilling life, which happens to be just as simple and straightforward as Abraham Maslow's quote, but so infrequently lived by as well:

"Do What Makes You Feel Good"

Many schools of thought may argue this statement by saying, for example, that feelings or emotions are temporary or transitory, so we should not base our actions on them; we should not base our actions or inactions on our internal state.

I tried on this train of thought and it certainly brought about beneficial outcomes; it taught me that my mind can be tricky and that I am often a lot more capable of performing than I thought I was or that I gave myself credit for. However, I discovered a glitch in that approach as it affects me personally, because -due to my sometimes rigid way of thinking- I used to be very hard on myself when for some reason I simply could not (emotionally speaking) get myself to do something.

In the chapter named Learning to Listen to Our Bodies I also mentioned how, in a few different instances in my life, I moved forward with something that 'did not feel good' -whether it was continuing to study in Israel when what I wanted was to travel or agreeing to requests from

168

people when they did not really work for me- and it undoubtedly contributed to me slipping into depression.

I know that there is no one-size-fits all or absolute approach that guarantees living a fulfilling life, but this is the closest to it for me. The moment I started deliberately gagging my choices based on "what felt good", my life turned around.

In 2016 I finally started traveling, which is what I had wanted to do since 2005, and I ended up moving to a very unexpected country and being the happiest and most fulfilled I had ever been anywhere. Around the same time, I allowed myself to start exploring my sexuality more freely, which I had wanted to do since my teenage years, but I did not have the courage to do. Through this freedom I discovered things about sexuality, about myself and about the world that I was completely fascinated by. I made life choices that resulted in the end of my former relationship, but that gave me access to learning to set healthy boundaries and to enter an extraordinarily loving and respectful relationship thereafter.

It really is *that* simple; if I want my life to flow, I get to limit myself to only doing/pursuing/choosing things that make me feel good and stopping when they no longer do - or when I have found something that makes me feel even better-. This last statement can be open to misinterpretation, because by no means do I consider life's elements (including people) to be disposable. What I mean is that it is natural for our priorities or preferences to change over time, and that there is nothing wrong with adjusting our lives accordingly while having conversations with people who may directly or indirectly be impacted by that adjustment.

I am going to give you an example. When I was traveling, it felt SO good to get to know new places, new cultures, new people, to learn new things and have new and unexpected experiences every single day, so much so that I kept saying how I wanted to travel the world indefinitely. The idea of settling down somewhere was not attractive at all, and most definitely not in my plans. It was not something that 'felt good'; the mere thought of doing that was anxiety provoking. Thus, I was only signing six-month contracts at a time in Vietnam because I did not want to feel stuck. Two years later, after I had worked for eighteen months in Vietnam and traveled around the world for the last six, it 'felt good' to sign an eighteen-month work contract in Vietnam because I loved my life there and it still gave me the freedom to travel pretty regularly.

It 'felt good' to have Vietnam as my base, and sort of settle down there; but the thought of doing that in Mexico did not feel good at all. A year later, and due to the worldwide circumstances of the pandemic, I ended up being somehow forced to turn Mexico into my base, because I had traveled there to visit my family but then the borders in Vietnam closed, and have remained closed since March 2020. The first three months my five-week trip extended for, I was on a happy vacation; but when I realized that I would not be able to go back, the happiness ceased (temporarily).

It was once I started *seeing* all the blessings that were coming to my life as a result of this situation, -the opportunity to develop a project with my brother, to see my immediate family regularly, to meet my girlfriend and have a beautiful relationship with her, to find out what my biological state in terms of reproduction was and being able to take action accordingly, amongst many others- being back in Mexico started to 'feel good'. Would I love to be traveling indefinitely right now? For sure! Do I still rather have the blessing to forge a wonderful future and a family right now, within which traveling will certainly be pursued as soon as it is possible? Absolutely! Both options 'feel good', but the latter feels even better for the given moment.

A couple of weeks ago I was having a conversation with my girlfriend about how, even though we have been together 24/7 for the past five months or so, we are still in the process of getting to know each other. Being reminded of this fact, I was able to communicate this "feeling good" matter to her as a crucial one in how I operate, in such a way that she could now understand why I seem to change my mind sometimes, because she used to be slightly bothered by that. In the past, I would have felt bad about changing my mind knowing it was something that my partner was not too pleased with, but due to all the work I have put in over the years to get to *see* my own worth and to dare to set healthy boundaries, I was able to tell her that this idea of 'changing my mind based on whether something felt good or not' is simply the way I choose to function, and if she wanted to spend the rest of her life with me, she would have to be okay with it. She knows there is a commitment from me to always bring workability into the relationship, thus this last statement does *not* mean that things will always have to be the way I want them. But it does request a slight level of flexibility on her part.

For instance, a few months ago we watched a movie and we heard the name of a character that we both liked, and we said we would like to name our daughter that way. The more I started thinking about the name, the less I liked it, but I could tell she was still very fond of it. She has two female embryos frozen, one out of which that G-d willing will make it to term at some point, so I told her that whenever we had that baby girl, we could use that name (as opposed to not using it at all, or to using it if the one with my eggs were to be a girl). Her initial reaction was "you always change things on me". But then we had the above conversation, and she got how me agreeing to using the name for one of her embryos was a way for me to find a middle ground that *still felt good* for me too, versus forcing myself to doing something that did not.

Clearly, the whole paragraph above is still speculation because we don't know what the future holds in terms of how many babies we will have and what their names will be; I may even end up changing my mind again in terms of when to use that name, who knows? The whole point though, is that it was important for me that my partner knew that if something doesn't feel good, or it used to but it no longer does, It is essential for me to know that I can freely change my mind and I do not need to force myself to do anything I don't want to at any moment.

Another example was in terms of me getting married again. For a while I used to say that I would not, that I was clear on how having that piece of paper did not guarantee that we would stay together -because it clearly had not happened both previous times-. The idea of getting married again did not 'feel good', however, as our relationship has progressed and I have continued to evolve, I was able to distinguish how, in this case, the papers will make a difference, not regarding whether we will stay together for the rest of our lives (which I am hoping to be the case), but yes regarding her having the same legal rights over our kids as I will. I want to create a family, and to have our kids have two phenomenal mothers. In order for that to legally happen, marriage is necessary; and knowing that this is the commitment behind the action definitely 'feels good'.

I have a friend who always says that *"there is never a dull moment in my life"*. I happen to agree with her, and I believe that what's behind that statement is an incessant willingness to flow with life and be as happy and fulfilled as possible at any given moment, giving up my attachment to things having to be -or continue being- a particular way. I strongly believe we can begin to thoroughly enjoy life the moment we learn to embrace its *impermanence*.

Now that you have read this far, you can understand the "why" behind the name of this book: Evolving Passerby. There is a word that profoundly describes its overall essence: the word SONDER.

Sonder is *"the realization that each random passerby is living a life as vivid and complex as your own - populated with their own ambitions, friends, routines, worries and inherited craziness-. An epic story that continues invisibly around you like an anthill, sprawling deep underground, with elaborate passageways to thousands of other lives that you'll never know existed, in which you might appear only once as an extra, sipping coffee in the background, as a blur of traffic passing on the highway, as a lighted window at dusk"*.

Just like Abraham Maslow, Abraham Hicks, Neale Donald Walsch, Jim Kwik, Lisa Nichols, Don Miguel Ruiz, Diego Dreyfus, my friend Brandy and all the other people I quoted are random passers-by in my life from whom I got something that has shifted an aspect of the way I live, I am one in yours; I live a life as vivid and complex as your own, with my own ambitions, friends, routines, worries and inherited craziness. Through reading this book, you are shedding light to that formerly-invisible story of mine, from which you can extract things that you would like to bring into your own life, or the clarity around things that you certainly would not want to. I may appear only once in your life, which is right now, while you are reading this book. Or it may be that, whatever you got out of entering into my world causes a shift in you, that will -even if slightly- permanently alter the way you experience life, in which case I would say that I'll stay with you forever, just like all these people have stayed with me.

However, this last statement applies to *anyone* you ever interact with - not only writers or public figures- and anyone who ever interacts with *you,* especially when vulnerability is present. I, personally, consider our lives to be a beautiful tapestry of all the interconnections we have throughout all of it, and there is a different word that encompasses this idea, which is *UBUNTU - I am because You are.*

May you always live a blessed and fulfilling life that is in complete alignment with Who You Are.

ACKNOWLEDGMENTS

There are infinite passers-by that contributed to the realization of this book, because as I said before, Who I Am and who I am constantly Becoming are nothing but the result of all my interactions. Thus, if you are reading this part - and whether we have met directly yet or not - I acknowledge you for making my life an extraordinary experience, and one worth writing about.

More specifically, I first of all thank G-d for having given me the life and strength to get through everything I have gotten through with such growth and gratitude, followed by providing me with the courage and confidence to share it with the world today.

I acknowledge Landmark's Team Management and Leadership Program (and everyone involved in it) for having been the space where I created myself as a writer and declared that this book would exist; Giovanna Molina for having consistently stood for me to dare to explore further and for my story to be told; and all those friends who over the years engaged in empowering conversations with me regarding the book.

To those of you who have shared - or who will share -your stories as a result of me opening up: I acknowledge your vulnerability and know that it encourages me to keep going.

To my family and loved ones: thank you for always being by my side and cheering me on.

I Love You, Always